BRITANNIA RULES

⊶ THE LOCHLAINN SEABROOK COLLECTION ⊷

AMERICAN CIVIL WAR
Abraham Lincoln Was a Liberal, Jefferson Davis Was a Conservative: The Missing Key to Understanding the American Civil War
Confederacy 101: Amazing Facts You Never Knew About America's Oldest Political Tradition
Confederate Blood and Treasure: An Interview With Lochlainn Seabrook
Everything You Were Taught About African-Americans and the Civil War is Wrong, Ask a Southerner!
Everything You Were Taught About the Civil War is Wrong, Ask a Southerner!
Give This Book to a Yankee! A Southern Guide to the Civil War For Northerners
Lincoln's War: The Real Cause, the Real Winner, the Real Loser
The Great Yankee Coverup: What the North Doesn't Want You to Know About Lincoln's War!
The Ultimate Civil War Quiz Book: How Much Do You Really Know About America's Most Misunderstood Conflict?
Women in Gray: A Tribute to the Ladies Who Supported the Southern Confederacy

CONFEDERATE MONUMENTS
Confederate Monuments: Why Every American Should Honor Confederate Soldiers and Their Memorials

CONFEDERATE FLAG
Confederate Flag Facts: What Every American Should Know About Dixie's Southern Cross
What the Confederate Flag Means to Me: Americans Speak Out in Defense of Southern Honor, Heritage, and History

SECESSION
All We Ask Is To Be Let Alone: The Southern Secession Fact Book

SLAVERY
Everything You Were Taught About American Slavery is Wrong, Ask a Southerner!
Slavery 101: Amazing Facts You Never Knew About America's "Peculiar Institution"

CHILDREN
Honest Jeff and Dishonest Abe: A Southern Children's Guide to the Civil War
Saddle, Sword, and Gun: A Biography of Nathan Bedford Forrest For Teens

NATHAN BEDFORD FORREST
A Rebel Born: A Defense of Nathan Bedford Forrest - Confederate General, American Legend (winner of the 2011 Jefferson Davis Historical Gold Medal)
A Rebel Born: The Screenplay (film about N. B. Forrest)
Forrest! 99 Reasons to Love Nathan Bedford Forrest
Give 'Em Hell Boys! The Complete Military Correspondence of Nathan Bedford Forrest
I Rode With Forrest! Confederate Soldiers Who Served With the World's Greatest Cavalry Leader
Nathan Bedford Forrest and African-Americans: Yankee Myth, Confederate Fact
Nathan Bedford Forrest and the Battle of Fort Pillow: Yankee Myth, Confederate Fact
Nathan Bedford Forrest and the Ku Klux Klan: Yankee Myth, Confederate Fact
Nathan Bedford Forrest: Southern Hero, American Patriot - Honoring a Confederate Icon and the Old South
Saddle, Sword, and Gun: A Biography of Nathan Bedford Forrest For Teens
The God of War: Nathan Bedford Forrest As He Was Seen By His Contemporaries
The Quotable Nathan Bedford Forrest: Selections From the Writings and Speeches of the Confederacy's Most Brilliant Cavalryman

QUOTABLE SERIES
The Alexander H. Stephens Reader: Excerpts From the Works of a Confederate Founding Father
The Quotable Alexander H. Stephens: Selections From the Writings and Speeches of the Confederacy's First Vice President
The Quotable Jefferson Davis: Selections From the Writings and Speeches of the Confederacy's First President
The Quotable Nathan Bedford Forrest: Selections From the Writings and Speeches of the Confederacy's Most Brilliant Cavalryman
The Quotable Robert E. Lee: Selections From the Writings and Speeches of the South's Most Beloved Civil War General
The Quotable Stonewall Jackson: Selections From the Writings and Speeches of the South's Most Famous General
The Unquotable Abraham Lincoln: The President's Quotes They Don't Want You To Know!

CIVIL WAR BATTLES
Encyclopedia of the Battle of Franklin - A Comprehensive Guide to the Conflict that Changed the Civil War
Nathan Bedford Forrest and the Battle of Fort Pillow: Yankee Myth, Confederate Fact
The Battle of Franklin: Recollections of Confederate and Union Soldiers
The Battle of Nashville: Recollections of Confederate and Union Soldiers
The Battle of Spring Hill: Recollections of Confederate and Union Soldiers

CONSTITUTIONAL HISTORY
The Articles of Confederation Explained: A Clause-by-Clause Study of America's First Constitution
The Constitution of the Confederate States of America Explained: A Clause-by-Clause Study of the South's Magna Carta

VICTORIAN CONFEDERATE LITERATURE
Rise Up and Call Them Blessed: Victorian Tributes to the Confederate Soldier, 1861-1901
The God of War: Nathan Bedford Forrest As He Was Seen By His Contemporaries
The Old Rebel: Robert E. Lee As He Was Seen By His Contemporaries
Victorian Confederate Poetry: The Southern Cause in Verse, 1861-1901

ABRAHAM LINCOLN
Abraham Lincoln: The Southern View - Demythologizing America's Sixteenth President
Lincolnology: The Real Abraham Lincoln Revealed in His Own Words - A Study of Lincoln's Suppressed, Misinterpreted, and Forgotten Writings and Speeches
Lincoln's War: The Real Cause, the Real Winner, the Real Loser
The Great Impersonator! 99 Reasons to Dislike Abraham Lincoln
The Unholy Crusade: Lincoln's Legacy of Destruction in the American South
The Unquotable Abraham Lincoln: The President's Quotes They Don't Want You To Know!

NATURAL HISTORY
North America's Amazing Mammals: An Encyclopedia for the Whole Family
The Concise Book of Owls: A Guide to Nature's Most Mysterious Birds
The Concise Book of Tigers: A Guide to Nature's Most Remarkable Cats

PARANORMAL
Carnton Plantation Ghost Stories: True Tales of the Unexplained from Tennessee's Most Haunted Civil War House!
UFOs and Aliens: The Complete Guidebook

FAMILY HISTORIES
The Blakeneys: An Etymological, Ethnological, and Genealogical Study - Uncovering the Mysterious Origins of the Blakeney Family and Name
The Caudills: An Etymological, Ethnological, and Genealogical Study - Exploring the Name and National Origins of a European-American Family
The McGavocks of Carnton Plantation: A Southern History - Celebrating One of Dixie's Most Noble Confederate Families and Their Tennessee Home

MIND, BODY, SPIRIT
Autobiography of a Non-Yogi: A Scientist's Journey From Hinduism to Christianity (Dr. Amitava Dasgupta, with Lochlainn Seabrook)
Britannia Rules: Goddess-Worship in Ancient Anglo-Celtic Society - An Academic Look at the United Kingdom's Matricentric Spiritual Past
Christ Is All and In All: Rediscovering Your Divine Nature and the Kingdom Within
Christmas Before Christianity: How the Birthday of the "Sun" Became the Birthday of the "Son"
Jesus and the Gospel of Q: Christ's Pre-Christian Teachings As Recorded in the New Testament
Jesus and the Law of Attraction: The Bible-Based Guide to Creating Perfect Health, Wealth, and Happiness Following Christ's Simple Formula
Seabrook's Bible Dictionary of Traditional and Mystical Christian Doctrines
The Bible and the Law of Attraction: 99 Teachings of Jesus, the Apostles, and the Prophets
The Book of Kelle: An Introduction to Goddess-Worship and the Great Celtic Mother-Goddess Kelle, Original Blessed Lady of Ireland
The Goddess Dictionary of Words and Phrases: Introducing a New Core Vocabulary for the Women's Spirituality Movement

WOMEN
Aphrodite's Trade: The Hidden History of Prostitution Unveiled
Princess Diana: Modern Day Moon-Goddess - A Psychoanalytical and Mythological Look at Diana Spencer's Life, Marriage, and Death (with Dr. Jane Goldberg)
Women in Gray: A Tribute to the Ladies Who Suppo

REPRINTS
A Short History of the Confederate States of America (author Jefferson Davis; editor Lochlainn Seabrook)

Lochlainn Seabrook does not author books for fame and fortune, but for the love of writing and sharing his knowledge.

SeaRavenPress.com

BRITANNIA RULES

Goddess-Worship in Ancient Anglo-Celtic Society

AN ACADEMIC LOOK AT THE UNITED KINGDOM'S
MATRICENTRIC SPIRITUAL PAST

LOCHLAINN SEABROOK
JEFFERSON DAVIS HISTORICAL GOLD MEDAL WINNER

Diligently Researched for the Elucidation of the Reader

2020

Sea Raven Press, Nashville, Tennessee, USA

BRITANNIA RULES

Published by
Sea Raven Press, Cassidy Ravensdale, President
PO Box 1484, Spring Hill, Tennessee 37174-1484 USA
SeaRavenPress.com • searavenpress@gmail.com

Copyright © text and illustrations Lochlainn Seabrook 1999, 2010, 2020
in accordance with U.S. and international copyright laws and regulations, as stated and protected under the Berne Union for the Protection of Literary and Artistic Property (Berne Convention), and the Universal Copyright Convention (the UCC). All rights reserved under the Pan-American and International Copyright Conventions.

1st SRP paperback edition, 1st printing, January 1999 • ISBN: 0976870738
2nd SRP paperback edition, 1st printing, June 2010 • ISBN: 978-0-9827700-2-3
2nd SRP paperback edition, 2nd printing, October 2020 • ISBN: 978-0-9827700-2-3
1st SRP hardcover edition, 1st printing, October 2020 • ISBN: 978-1-943737-91-8

ISBN: 978-0-9827700-2-3 (paperback)
Library of Congress Control Number: 2010929565

This work is the copyrighted intellectual property of Lochlainn Seabrook and has been registered with the Copyright Office at the Library of Congress in Washington, D.C., USA. No part of this work (including text, covers, drawings, photos, illustrations, maps, images, diagrams, etc.), in whole or in part, may be used, reproduced, stored in a retrieval system, or transmitted, in any form or by any means now known or hereafter invented, without written permission from the publisher. The sale, duplication, hire, lending, copying, digitalization, or reproduction of this material, in any manner or form whatsoever, is also prohibited, and is a violation of federal, civil, and digital copyright law, which provides severe civil and criminal penalties for any violations.

Britannia Rules: Goddess-Worship in Ancient Anglo-Celtic Society - An Academic Look at the United Kingdom's Matricentric Spiritual Past, by Lochlainn Seabrook. Includes bibliographical references and index.

Front and back cover design and art, book design, layout, and interior art by Lochlainn Seabrook.
All images, graphic design, graphic art, and illustrations copyright © Lochlainn Seabrook.
All images selected, placed, manipulated, and/or created by Lochlainn Seabrook.
Front cover photo: "Calanais Standing Stones," Callanish, Isle of Lewis, Scotland, © Billy Currie.

Printed and manufactured in occupied Tennessee, former Confederate States of America

DEDICATION

To an Anglo-Celtic Goddess.

EPIGRAPH

" . . . the great Goddess . . . whom all Asia and the world worshippeth."

SAINT PAUL (ACTS 19:27)

CONTENTS

"Rule Britannia!" (lyrics) - 11
Notes to the Reader - 13
Introduction - 21

1 Anglo-Celtic Goddess-Worship in the Prehistoric Period - 27
2 The Iberians and the Henges - 31
3 Albion and the Celtic Moon-Worshipers - 37
4 The Fire-Goddess Brigid: The Original Trinity - 41
5 The Romans and Britannia - 45
6 The Germans and Frigga - 51
7 Goddess in Scotland - 57
8 Goddess Across Europe - 65
9 Goddess in Ireland - 71
10 The Celts and the Goddess Kelle - 81
11 The Cow-Goddesses - 85
12 Saint Bridget and the Virgin Mary - 87
13 Ancient Remnants of Goddess-Worship in Modern England - 101
14 Britannia Rules - 105
15 Goddess-ography - 107

Bibliography - 115
Index - 147
Meet the Author - 197
Meet the Cover Photographer - 199
Learn More - 201

Keep Your Body, Mind, & Spirit Vibrating at Their Highest Level

YOU CAN DO SO BY READING THE BOOKS OF

SEA RAVEN PRESS

There is nothing that will so perfectly keep your body, mind, and spirit in a healthy condition as to think wisely and positively. Hence you should not only read this book, but also the other books that we offer. They will quicken your physical, mental, and spiritual vibrations, enabling you to maintain a position in society as a healthy erudite person.

KEEP YOURSELF WELL-INFORMED!

The well-informed person is always at the head of the procession, while the ignorant, the lazy, and the unthoughtful hang onto the rear. If you are a Spiritual man or woman, do yourself a great favor: read Sea Raven Press books and stay well posted on the Truth. It is almost criminal for one to remain in ignorance while the opportunity to gain knowledge is open to all at a nominal price.

We invite you to visit our Webstore for a wide selection of wholesome, family-friendly, well-researched, educational books for all ages. You will be glad you did!

Five-Star Books & Gifts From the Heart of the American South

SeaRavenPress.com

RULE BRITANNIA!

Britain's Unofficial National Anthem
LYRICS: JAMES THOMSON (1700-1748)

Rule Britannia!
When Britain first, at Heaven's command
Arose from out the azure main
Arose from out the azure main
This was the charter, the charter of the land
And guardian angels sang this strain

Chorus
Rule Britannia! Britannia rules the waves
Britons never, never, never shall be slaves

The nations, not so blest as thee
Must, in their turns to tyrants fall
Must, in their turns to tyrants fall
While thou shalt flourish, shalt flourish great and free
The dread and envy of them all
(Chorus)

Still more majestic shalt thou rise
More dreadful from each foreign stroke
More dreadful from each foreign stroke
As the loud blast, the blast that tears the skies
Serves but to root thy native oak.
(Chorus)

Thee haughty tyrants ne'er shall tame
All their attempts to bend thee down
All their attempts to bend thee down
Will but arouse, arouse thy generous flame
But work their woe, and thy renown.
(Chorus)

To thee belongs the rural reign
Thy cities shall with commerce shine
Thy cities shall with commerce shine
All thine shall be, shall be the subject main
And every shore it circles thine
(Chorus)

The Muses, still with freedom found
Shall to thy happy coast repair
Shall to thy happy coast repair
Blest isle with matchless, with matchless beauty crowned
And manly hearts to guard the fair
(Chorus)

NOTES TO THE READER

☞ The names of the goddesses mentioned herein are set apart in small caps for ease of reference. For example, the War-Goddess BRITANNIA.

☞ I have entitled this study of European Goddess-worship, *Britannia Rules*. This is not meant, however, to show preference for England or Great Britain—or even Europe for that matter. I view all female divinities on equal footing. Thus, I could have just as easily named my book *Éire Rules* (after the goddess who gave her name to Ireland), or any one of the hundreds of other feminine native European immortals.

Britannia is merely a convenient and familiar female deity name that I am using here as a general European goddess archetype. For all the major (and many of the minor) European goddesses are but embodiments of the universal Mother-Goddess (or of her various characteristics), known around the globe by thousands of different names.

☞ So many readers have asked me about my genealogy that I have taken the liberty of including some of my more ancient genealogical connections in the footnotes.

☛ Though I feel it is unfortunate that certain early male-dominant groups found it necessary to undermine female spirituality, and even seek to completely eliminate female religion and its many feminine accoutrements, I am not anti-patriarchy. Indeed, history

shows that much if not most of human society (European, Asian, American, and African) was built and developed by patriarchal peoples. Thus while I honor our matriarchal ancestors and their numerous contributions to our world, one cannot overlook the planet-altering achievements made by the patriarchalists who came before us. Without these sagacious rugged men and women, much of what we take for granted today would not exist.

☛ After perusing this book, some readers might think I am anti-religion, or at the very least anti-Christian. Actually I am both pro-religion and a Christian, and in fact, these are just two of the many reasons that the topic of Goddess-worship interests me.

But being a Christian, some might ask, how can I pen a book about Goddess-worship which often seems to refute many traditional Christian beliefs and doctrines?

The idea of a female Supreme Being (alone or as the wife of a male Supreme Being) is not at variance with original Christianity, which began as a Gnostic-Jewish faith steeped in Pagan beliefs, rituals, and mythology (the ideas of baptism, prayer, fasting, sacrament, holy days, tithing, sin and atonement, the divine son, the virgin mother, for example, all originated with Paganism and can be found in the records of religions thousands of years older than Christianity).[1]

One of the predominant beliefs in the pre-Christian world was the concept of the Great Mother-Goddess, who gave birth to the Universe and all life, and who nurtures her children with her unconditional maternal love.

In an effort to win Pagan converts, the Christian Church—both the original (mystical or Gnostic) branch and the later developing orthodox (Ecclesiastical or Catholic) branch—adopted and christianized many of the accouterments of Paganism. One of these was the notion of an all-powerful divine female.

To this day, numerous Christian denominations, among them the Gnostics, the Mormons, and the Shakers, continue to actively embrace the idea of a feminine Deity, while some, like the Quakers and the Unitarians, do not oppose it.

The Catholic Church, while not officially endorsing this specific idea, continues to promote the veneration of the Virgin Mary, a

---

1. For more on this topic see my book, *Christmas Before Christianity: How the Birthday of the "Sun" Became the Birthday of the "Son."*

Western personification of the pre-Christian Mother-Goddess, known variously among the world's many religions and myths as Ma, Ma Ma, Mar, Mara, Marah, Maria, Mariam, Maerin, Meri, Myrrha, Kel-Mari, and Maid Marian, to name but a few.[2]

The need for a divine mother is deeply ingrained in us, both psychologically and biologically. Modern studies, for instance, reveal that the worship of Mary is much stronger among Catholics than the worship of Jesus, much to the consternation of Church authorities. In fact, in response to the laity's universal love of Mary, many Catholic Churches display a statue of Mary outside their doors rather than one of Jesus. As the Christian Church is named after our Savior, this is a rather curious practice indeed.

Attraction toward the Divine Feminine is more popular than that toward the Divine Masculine in other religions as well, such as Hinduism and Wicca.

Truly the idea of a "Heavenly Mother" seems to be inherent to the human psyche, which is, no doubt, why the earliest religious icons found in the archaeological record are of female deities rather than male ones.

We will note here that the most ancient words for "spirit" in a

---

[2]. For more on this topic see my work, *The Book of Kelle: An Introduction to Goddess-Worship and the Great Celtic Mother-Goddess Kelle, Original Blessed Lady of Ireland*.

majority of languages are feminine, not masculine. Little wonder then that the idea of a female Supreme Being has played an integral role in the mystical branches of all religions, including Christianity, the wing of the faith to which I adhere.

I am not alone. Pope John Paul II, Julian of Norwich, Irenaeus, Saint Hildegard, Thomas Aquinas, Tertullian, Saint Polycarp, Francis of Assisi, Martin Luther, Saint John of the Cross, Origen, Bernard of Clairvaux, Meister Eckhart, Thomas Merton, Catherine of Siena, Saint Paul, and Saint Augustine, all counted themselves Christian mystics. Some of these individuals, like hundreds of millions around the world, also embraced a belief in the Divine Feminine in one form or another. The English anchoress Julian of Norwich, for example, referred to Jesus as "our precious Mother" and "God our Mother."

As the mystic Saint Paul preached, in the mystical Christian tradition not only do we respect other faiths and beliefs (even if they diverge completely from our own),[3] but we seek to maintain an openness to other, even opposing, ideas in a constant effort to learn and grow in both knowledge and in spirit. For it is written, "except ye be . . . as little children, ye shall not enter into the kingdom of heaven."[4]

---

3. Romans 14:1-10.
4. Matthew 18:3.

Those who possess the open, questioning, childlike mind taught by Jesus will perceive an obvious truth, one espoused by Saint Paul and other Christians thousands of years ago: the Supreme Being of Paganism and the Supreme Being of Christianity are one and the same.[5] Jews and Muslims, who share the Bible as a holy book, also venerate this same great divinity, though this wonderful truth is sadly often lost amidst today's cultural and religious tensions, misunderstandings, and prejudice.

Intriguingly, throughout the Bible the Supreme Being is portrayed in a variety of forms and genders. Though best known as a male,[6] it is also depicted as an androgynous being, half-male, half-female;[7] as a polytheistic group of deities, the *Elohim*;[8] and more importantly for us, as a female.[9]

As early as the second verse of Genesis, God is said to "*brood* upon the face of the waters" (the word brood here is commonly, and intentionally, mistranslated by patriarchal scholars as "moved"). But brooding or incubating—that is, sitting upon a nest of eggs—is typically a female attribute, not a male one.

During Saint Paul's day, belief in the Mother-Goddess (who, in one of her many guises, was venerated across the Roman Empire as the

---

5. See e.g., Acts 17: 22-23.
6. Matthew 6:14.
7. Genesis 1:27.
8. Genesis 1:26; 3:22.
9. See e.g., Psalms 48:3; Job 38:29.

Goddess Diana) was far more popular than the Father-God, by both Pagans and Christians. In fact, her religion was worldwide at the time, as the beloved saint himself noted in the book of Acts.[10] It was only later, when sexist androcentric Church authorities censored the Christian idea of the Divine Feminine,[11] that mainstream Christianity began worshiping a single male Supreme Being.

Belief in the many forms of the Mother-Goddess, however, is still very much alive and well throughout Christian Great Britain (and all across Europe in fact), as we will see.

It is my hope that readers of *Britannia Rules* will find the topic of European Goddess-worship as fascinating and enlightening as I and millions of others do. It is a complex but worthwhile subject, one that can only enrich one's present beliefs, whatever they may be.

L.S.

---

10. Acts 19:27,
11. This process began among the Jews early on; see e.g., 1 Kings 11:31-33; 15:9-13.

INTRODUCTION

England, Scotland, Wales, and Ireland have been androcentric Christian nations for so many centuries that it is difficult to imagine that they were ever otherwise. Indeed, if we are to believe "conventional wisdom," the religious tradition of the British Isles is, and always has been, a patriarchal monotheistic worship of an all-male Trinity, with a fatherly God at its head.

As the epigraph in this book reveals, however, it is clear that 2,000 years ago the entire world was venerating, not a *male* Supreme Being, but a *female* one. This fact was so manifestly obvious at the time that even Saint Paul, Christianity's most important Apostle, recognized it *and* felt the need to report it to his followers.[12]

We should not be surprised at this. Paul, like the rest of his contemporaries, would have been fully aware of the universal nature of Goddess-worship throughout Europe and the Near-East, and he admitted as much.

What Paul probably did not realize, however, was that all Iron Age societies—such as the early Celts and Britons—were either originally completely matriarchal in character, or passed through a long matriarchal phase. Indeed, what he was

---

12. See Acts 19:27.

observing in the 1st Century was the tail-end of a pre-patriarchal, 500,000 year-old period known as the Goddess World, or more accurately, the Matriarchate: a global socioreligious culture based not around fathers and the Masculine Principle, but mothers and the Feminine Principle.

Naturally, matriarchal societies, being matricentric (mother-centered), instinctively image the Supreme Being as female, a deity known everywhere generically as "Goddess." This, in fact, makes female-based religion, and the Goddess-worship it was built upon, the United Kingdom's true religious tradition.

What *is* surprising is that many so-called British "experts" in the field of ancient religion are either wholly ignorant of the feminine-based spiritual belief systems that once permeated every acre of their verdant isles, or they actually deny that they ever existed there! In light of the overwhelming evidence for Goddess-worship in early Britain (the focus of this book), a reasoning person must ask the question "why"?

In ancient Anglo-Celtic society, sacred knowledge (*gnosis*) was not recorded in books as it is today: it was considered sacrosanct. Thus it was handed down orally, a custom that, for modern scholars and historians, has tended to obscure an already murky period in the United Kingdom's history.

Additionally, we have the problem of theology and science themselves, fields which, until recently, have been almost wholly male-dominated. (Indeed, thealogy, the scientific study of Goddess and female religion, has been virtually ignored in the West, and is only now beginning to make its presence known—as this book attests.)

And because men (and most women) in patriarchal societies tend to focus on the accomplishments of men while de-emphasizing those of women, the inevitable result has been a climate of male bias, one that has almost totally obliterated the United Kingdom's matricentric phase.[13]

All is not lost, however. Recent more objective scholarship has uncovered astonishing fresh details about Britain's authentic religious foundation, one rooted in the Divine Feminine.

Let us now explore this exciting new information and, without detracting from the sacred beliefs of male-dominant religions or of modern day Britain (as that is not my intention), set the record straight. Since this topic is so vast we will focus primarily on England.

LOCHLAINN SEABROOK
Franklin, Tennessee
Summer Solstice 2010

---

13. Unfortunately, this same process, the patriarchalization of religion, has occurred in most other nations and among most other peoples as well, effectively eliminating nearly all traces of a once flourishing worldwide female-oriented spiritual belief system.

BRITANNIA RULES

GODDESS-WORSHIP IN
ANCIENT ANGLO-CELTIC SOCIETY

1

ANGLO-CELTIC GODDESS-WORSHIP IN THE PREHISTORIC PERIOD

The famed early 20th-Century Scottish scholar J. A. MacCulloch writes that there was a time when the early inhabitants of the British Isles worshiped "goddesses rather than gods." While this fact may be news to many modern-day academicians, it was already well established thousands of years ago.

Ancient historians, such as Strabo, Diodorus, Julius Caesar, Pliny the Elder, Tacitus,[14] Ptolemy, Cassius Dio, and Ammianus Marcellinus, for example, all described in intimate detail the predominance of female-based religions in England

---

14. Tacitus "of the Red Robe" is my 40th great-grandfather.

during pre-Christian times.

According to these classical authorities, all of the British Isles were once matriarchal in nature and their occupants worshiped the Supreme Being in female form; a great Mother-Goddess who went by a myriad of local and regional names.

As archaeologist Marija Gimbutas and many other scientists have shown, the fossil record supports this view. Britain's earliest inhabitants, the Paleolithic hominids known as *Homo erectus*—who began migrating into England by at least 500,000 years ago—brought with them overt signs of an already flourishing Goddess religion: crudely-made flint carvings of female figures. Revealingly, archaeologists have not uncovered any corresponding male figures from this time period.

Homo erectus was followed by three other Goddess-worshiping groups: the Neanderthals; archaic *Homo sapiens*; and the Cro-Magnon people.

These three groups left behind such obvious Goddess-oriented items as three-sided stones (representing the GREAT MOTHER'S pubic triangle—"the source of all life") and stunningly sophisticated sculptures of archetypal females, the famed VENUS statues, with their faceless heads, large swollen breasts, pregnant abdomens, wide flaring hips, and huge buttocks.

Again, no comparable male figurines have ever been found in the remains of Lower, Middle, or Upper Paleolithic peoples.

The Iberians and the Henges

The next group to make Britain their home, the Neolithic Iberians (who migrated into the British Isles some 4,000 years ago from France, Spain, and North Africa), were Goddess-worshipers as well. As incontrovertible proof, they left behind some 1,000 stone and wood henges scattered across the rolling landscapes of England and Wales.

Modern mainstream scientists, unfamiliar with, or hostile to, England's deep-seated feminine spiritual tradition, have long believed that these monuments were either secular administrative structures or the royal tombs of male chieftains.

In truth, they were Iberian religious shrines dedicated to the worship of Goddess; sanctuaries that served as sites for Lunar and Solar observations, dance, ritual, sports, games, funerals, meetings, and festivals, held in her honor.

The geographical location of many of England's henge monuments is connected to another aspect of Goddess-worship: crop circles. Ancient Goddess-worshiping Britons would certainly have seen such mysterious wind-generated rings as sacred manifestations of Goddess' mighty power, and so would have built round monuments over them.

As a circular monument created by Moon-worshiping designers (a phase known as "Stonehenge I," c. 5000 BCE) who aligned the axis of the site with the Moonrise, Stonehenge is unquestionably one of the more obvious examples of matricentric religion in early England.

Depth psychology reveals that all egg-shaped, round, curved, and elliptical patterns and formations are female breast, womb, and regeneration symbols, which connects them with the Feminine Principle and, in the context of Stonehenge, with Goddess-worship.

Hence we can see the logic behind the monument's striking circuitous shape, a shape that suggests the life-nurturing female breast, or possibly the pregnant abdomen, of the Celtic Britons' great Mother-Goddess BRIGANTIA.

Stonehenge reveals other signs of an ancient female-based spiritual belief system as well. For instance, at its center there are two U-shaped formations of upright stones: an inner and outer horseshoe. Due to its shape the horseshoe has long been a symbol of both Goddess' crescent Moon and the Holy Yoni (the female vulva), itself an all-encompassing emblem signifying entrances and exits, beginnings and endings, birth and death.

The inner horseshoe at Stonehenge is particularly indicative of Goddess-worship: it contains nineteen standing stones, the exact number of both BRIGANTIA'S priestesses and of the years in the Celtic "Great Year," a period governed by Goddess herself.

We will note here that in sacred numerology, nineteen equals one (1 + 9 = 10, and 1 + 0 = 1), one being the archetypal number equated with bounteous fortune, feminine energy, and the Supreme Being.

Like England's ancient Druids, many contemporary Britons,

though unwittingly, still practice the ancient custom of honoring Goddess by hanging horseshoes above their doors for "good luck."

The nineteen standing stones of Stonehenge must also be connected to what we now call the Major Lunar Standstill, an event that occurs every nineteen years (specifically 18.61 years). Always occurring near an equinox, the Major Lunar Standstill mimics the Solstice in June at which time the Sun travels its most northern path and appears to "stand still." In the Northern hemisphere the Major Lunar Standstill marks the Moon's most northern path, while in the Southern hemisphere it marks the Moon's most southern path.

Such significant Lunar events have always played an important role in human societies. As such, ancient Britons built many henges to correlate with the Major Lunar Standstill.

One obvious example is the famed Stone Ring of Callanish, on Scotland's Ilse of Lewis, a hauntingly beautiful matricentric monument shown on the cover of this book. Built some 5,400 years ago, the main ring is composed of thirteen standing stones (associated with the thirteen-month Lunar Calendar of the Goddess religion), and is aligned to function as an astronomical calendar that accurately delineates the nineteen-year cycle of the Major Lunar Standstill.

Nearby is a group of hills that look like a giant woman lying on her back. Known by the English as "Sleeping Beauty" and by the Scots as *Cailleach na Mointeach* ("Old Woman of the Moors"), this feature, along with these names, shows the ancient connection between the island's matricentric monument, Lunar beliefs, and Goddess-worship—an intensely powerful female-based religiosity dating back hundreds of thousands of years.

But the Standing Stones of Callanish (only one of some twenty feminine megalithic structures in the area) were designed to be more than a mere calendar to plot the course of the Moon. This sacred temple site, where the radiation level has been shown to double during Solstices, has long been considered by the Scottish people to be an ideal spot for couples to perform the ancient feminine rite known as the *Hieros Gamos* ("Sacred Union"), which unites the two genders in physical and spiritual oneness.[15]

---

15. Contrary to mainstream medical teaching, small doses of radiation have been shown to provide numerous health benefits. Knowledge of this form of therapy, known as radiation hormesis, was almost certainly possessed by the ancients. Radiation hormesis has experienced a recent resurgence of interest, and, despite the usual resistance of the mainstream medical establishment, has been shown to be highly effective by such scientists as Thomas D. Luckey.

3

ALBION AND THE CELTIC MOON-WORSHIPERS

We have far more than just archeological evidence for early matriarchal Goddess-worship in what is now the United Kingdom, however. Even more revealing is modern England's toponymy (place-names).

Ancient writers tell us that among the first recorded inhabitants of England were the Albiones, a Celtic tribe who arrived sometime after 600 BCE.

It was the Albiones who, in the 5th Century BCE, gave England her first known name: Albion. The Romans later mistakenly connected the word Albion with the masculine Latin word *albus* ("white"), as a reference to the white cliffs of Dover.

In reality, as the Christian monk Bede reluctantly pointed out, ALBION was the name of the Celts' all-important Mother-

Moon-Goddess (Albion means "White-face" or "White Moon"), which is why they named both themselves and their territory after her (Albiones means the "followers of [the Goddess] ALBION").

In Wales Albion was called CERRIDWEN, a Celtic Triple-Muse-Goddess, also known as "the White Lady of Death" (*cerdd* is an Irish-Welsh word loosely meaning "inspirational arts"; *wen* is the Gaelic word for white).

ALBION herself has a fascinating history, one dating from at least ancient Greece, where she was known as the Goddess ALPHITO, the eldest of King Danaus' fifty daughters, THE DANAIDS, the Ancestor-Goddess of the Argive tribe known as the Danai. (Later British legends would portray her as the mortal but fanciful "Princess Albia, oldest of fifty daughters of the King of Syria," said to have fled her native land, eventually settling in Britain.)

In ancient Rome ALBION was called ALBINA, a name, like ALPHITO, which literally means "the White Goddess."

One of the Goddess' primary shrines in ancient England was at Holmhurst Hill, the site of her sacred fountain. When

Christians took over the region centuries later, ALBION was both Christianized and masculinized, becoming the fictitious "Saint Alban," conveniently said to have been "martyred" on Holmhurst Hill in the year 287.

London's Tower Hill was also one of ALBION'S sacred sites, as revealed in its original name: the White Hill.

ALBION'S influence once spread far and wide across Europe. Germany's Elbe River, and the cities of Alba, Italy, and Albi, France, for example, were named after her, as was the small Balkan country of Albania (meaning "Land of the White Goddess").

We still honor this particular Moon-Goddess every Monday, her sacred day of the week: early Britons referred to this day as *Monandaeg*, or in modern English, "Moon's Day," a phrase that eventually became corrupted to Monday.

40 ∞ BRITANNIA RULES

The Fire-Goddess Brigid: The Original Trinity

By the beginning of the Common Era the Celts of England had renamed their land, as was the Celtic custom, after one of their own female deities. In this case it was the Fire-Goddess BRIGID or BRIDGIT, a great triple-deity whose name means "Bright Arrow" or the "Bright One," and whose triadic roles govern smithcraft, poetry, and healing.

It was in tribute to BRIGID that the Celts called their sprawling empire Brigantia, a region that included parts of the British Isles, France, and Spain.

BRIGID was Britain's first Holy Trinity, a divinity that took many forms. The most popular of these was the "three-in-one" Triple-Goddess, a deity known collectively in Ireland as

ANA-BADB-MACHA (that is, ANA, meaning "grace"; BADB, meaning "boiling"; and MACHA, meaning "Great Queen of Phantoms"). She was also known as THE MORRIGAN, the great Irish War-Goddess who frequented battlefields, selecting which soldiers would live and which would die, as she flew overhead.

The Druids ("Oak-Men") knew her as DIANA TRIFORMIS, while she appears in Shakespeare's *Macbeth* as the "three Weird Sisters."

Psychologically speaking, the Triple-Goddess archetype represents both the birth-life-death cycle and the mind-body-spirit complex. Ancient British and Irish artisans portrayed their Triple-Goddess as a virgin (the "Creatress"), a mother (the "Preserver"), and a grandmother or old wise crone (the "Destroyer").

While today the three-pointed Latin Cross (✚) is the best known religious symbol throughout the British Isles, to the early Celtic inhabitants of England it was the triple spiral (☘), an overtly feminine spiritual symbol signifying the eternal rhythm of life as perpetuated by the Triple-Goddess BRIGID.

Among the Celtic Britons, always preoccupied with defending themselves against new waves of combative invaders, BRIGID eventually became the War-Goddess BRIGANTIA (the "Strong Fighting One"), whose memory is preserved in the name of one of the many rivers she governed: the Brent in Middlesex.

Just as the famed Druidic Warrior-Queen of the Iceni, Boudicca,[16] offered sacrifice to the British War-Goddess ANDRASTE ("Invincible One") before battle, so did other early Celtic-Britons propitiate BRIGANTIA, not only in preparation for war, but also in time of sickness, and while working with metals and fire.

One British tribe, the Brigantes (led by the Warrior-Queen Cartimandua), named themselves after this military-goddess, centering their adoration of her in what is now Aldborough, Yorkshire—a city the Romans called *Isurium Brigantum*, revealing the ancient focus of this BRIGANTIA-worshiping region.[17] (Note that the place-name Aldborough itself harkens back to the time when BRIGANTIA the War-Goddess ruled the area: *eald* is the Old English word for "old," while *burh* is the Old English word for "stronghold"; thus meaning, "old fort [of

---

16. Queen Boudicca is my 40th great-grandmother.
17. *Isurium* derives from the Roman Latin word *isara*, meaning "strong river."

the Goddess BRIGANTIA].")

It is said that nineteen priestesses (representing the nineteen-year cycle of the Celtic "Great Year") tended an "Eternal Flame" or sacred fire in the Goddess' honor at her women-only shrine at Kildare, Ireland. (Kildare, as we will see, is named after the great Celtic Goddess KELLE, from whom the Celts themselves take their name.)

So deeply imbedded was the religion of BRIGID that despite the introduction of patriarchal Christianity in the 6th Century, this matriarchal ritual (of the Eternal Flame) persisted until the time of England's King Henry the VIII,[18] in the 16th Century. BRIGID'S reconstructed sanctuary can still be seen at Kildare.

---

18. King Henry VIII is my 4th cousin, 14 times removed.

The Romans and Britannia

Next, the Romans, who invaded Britain in the year 43 (under Emperor Claudius),[19] latinized BRIGID'S Celto-English name BRIGANTIA, calling her BRITANNIA, which in English later became the shortened anglicized form in use to this day: Britain.

In early Scotland BRIGID was called BRIDE (pronounced Breed), the source of our modern word bride (for every earthly woman is an aspect of the heavenly Mother-Goddess). In the area of Edinburgh BRIGID was also known as TRIDUANA (the "Three Dianas"), whose sacred places were wells located beneath oak trees.

Like so many other Goddesses before and after her, TRIDUANA

---

[19]. Emperor Claudius is my 41st great-grandfather.

was eventually christianized and transformed into a fictional saint; in this case "Saint Triduana." But this Goddess' Pagan influence persisted for centuries after in Scotland, and it was not until 1560 that her last Scottish holy shrine, at Restalrig, was torn down.

In early France, where BRIGID was known as BRIGANDU, she gave her name not only to the region of Brittany (in French, *Bretagne*), but also to its Celtic citizens, the Bretons, and to their Celtic language, Breton (a Middle English word derived from the Latin word *Brito* or *Briton*, which freely translated means "an inhabitant of the Land of the Goddess BRIGANTIA prior to the Anglo-Saxon invasions").

Other common words derive from the great Anglo-Celtic Goddess BRIGID-BRIGANTIA as well: brig, brigade, brigadier, brigand, and brigantine.

We have a number of additional indications that a female-based Goddess-worshiping religion once flourished as the original spiritual belief system in the British Isles.

London, for example, is a Middle English word meaning "fortress of the Moon," perhaps distantly from Lundonn (*lun*, "lunar," and *donn*, "power," "warrior," or "ruler"), an overt reference to the time when this city was governed by worshipers of the ubiquitous European Moon-Goddess. The surname Lundon is still a modern day Irish variant of the surname London.

The word London has affinities with the old Mesopotamian *lugal*, a title-word that the Celts used to signify the male spouse of the Earth-Goddess.

The Earth-Goddess of the Celts was TAILLTU (Taillten, Ireland, is named after her), while her *lugal* (mate) was the Celtic Sun-God and Savior-King Lug or Lud. Lug/Lud—the son of the Irish Goddess ETHNE ("sweet nutmeat"), Princess of the Irish Sea-Deities (the Formorians), and her male consort, the God Diancecht—was the patron male deity of the city now known as London, which is why the Romans called it *Lugdunum*, a name that was later anglicized, becoming Lundinium, and finally London.

Lug/Lud was sacrificed at Lud's Gate; not a gate at all, but rather one of TAILLTU'S sacred stones, one known as the *Crom Cruaich* (the "Bloody [Lunar] Crescent"). The stone stood at the gate to Lug's temple on a site still known today in London as Ludgate Hill.

Lug, who some claim was born of the Irish Virgin-Mother-Goddess DECHTERE, appeared in Irish myth as "King Lugadius" and later in Christian mythology as the spurious "Saint Lugad" or "Saint Lugidus." Some early myths state that Lug was the brother of the great Irish hero Cuchulain.

Even though the Romans were already by then a largely patriarchal culture who venerated the male Father-God Jupiter (also variously known among other peoples as Zeus, Jason, Jove, Jahweh, Yahweh, Jesus, and Jehovah),[20] they retained many elements of their earlier matriarchal phase, which included Goddess-worship.

Thus we find that the Romans' name for the city of Bath, England, was originally *Aquae Sulis* (the "waters of Sul"), named for the fact that Bath was then the site of a holy shrine dedicated to the great Celtic Water-Goddess SUL ("sun" or "eye"), known in her Triple-Goddess form as SULIVIAE. (Also venerated alongside SULIVIAE at Bath was the Water-Goddess

---

20. All of these god-names ultimately derive from the same etymological foundation: the Sanskrit word *dyaus*, "divine." To this word was later added *pitar*, "father," creating the full title *Dyaus Pitar*: "Divine Father." *Dyaus Pitar* is also sometimes rendered "Shining Father," "Shining God," "Sun Father," "Sun-God," or "Celestial Father." This Pagan god-title has more commonly come down to modern Christianity as "Heavenly Father." See e.g., Matthew 6:14, 26.

NEMETONA, "Goddess of the Sacred Grove.")

The Romans latinized SUL'S name (to SULIS) and blended her with their Wisdom-Goddess MINERVA, creating the important goddess known as SULIS-MINERVA.

SULIS-MINERVA appears in British-Celtic mythology as King Arthur's sister, the Death-Goddess MORGAN (Gaelic for "sea-white") LE FAY (French for "the Fate"); in Irish mythology as BLATHNAT ("Little Flower"); in Welsh mythology as the Virgin Spring-Goddess BLODEUWEDD (Welsh for "Flower-face"); and in Judeo-Christian mythology as DELILAH (Hebrew for the "Dainty Tease").

50 ∾ BRITANNIA RULES

6

The Germans and Frigga

Even after the final withdrawal of Roman troops from Britain in the year 410, the next wave of invaders to arrive on England's shores (c. mid-5th Century), the Germans, brought with them a continuing tradition of Goddess-worship. So strong was this belief system that they even named the month of March after a female deity; in this case, the Germanic Spring-Goddess RHEDA or HREDE. The name they gave the third month of what is now the Gregorian calendar was *Rhed-monat*, "Rheda's Month."

These particular Germanic tribes, the Jutes, the Saxons, and the Angles (whom the Romans called the *Angli*, because they looked like "angels"), venerated a powerful Sex- and Love-Goddess known as FRIGG or FRIGGA (meaning "She Who is Loved").

Known to Scandinavians as FREYA, to the Lombards as FREA, to the Romans as VENUS ("Sexual Love"), to the Welsh as BRANWEN or BRONWEN ("White-Bosomed One" or "White Crow"), and to the Greeks as APHRODITE (born "of the [Sea] Foam"), the German tribes honored their Goddess FRIGGA in sacred tree groves and at holy springs and wells.

FRIGGA'S sacred day fell on the sixth (or what used to be the seventh) day of the week, a day they called *Friatag*, that is, "FRIGGA'S Day."

In the Old English (that is, Anglo-Saxon) language of this period, the German word *Friatag* became *Frigedaeg*. The ancient Goddess-worshiping Scots maintained that FRIGGA'S Day was the ideal day for marriage, since she is also a goddess of fertility.

Centuries later—after all of England had adopted this holy day dedicated to FRIGGA—*Frigedaeg* became the Middle English word we still use for the sixth day of the week: Friday.

We will note that the ancient Romans called Friday *Dies Veneris*, or "Day of VENUS," after FRIGGA'S Latin counterpart VENUS, which is why Italians still refer to Friday as *Venerdì*, or

"VENUS' Day." Venus would later be "converted" by the Christian Church and transformed into the bogus "Saint Venerina" or "Saint Venere."

Finally, it was the Goddess-worshiping Angels (*Angli*), or rather the Angles (in Old English, *Engles*) who, after conquering Britain, gave their feminine name to the land: in English the German word *Angleslant* ("Engles' Land," that is, "Angel's Land") eventually became "England."

Every invader and immigrant to England's shores, it seems, brought with them some aspect of Goddess-worship, even the Gypsies (or Travelers), who descend from a proudly matriarchal Goddess-worshiping culture in Hindustan, where the great Triple-Goddess KALI MA ("Dark Mother") is still the most popular deity.

The depth of the Goddess tradition among the Travelers can still be seen in the name of their language, Romany, which derives from Rome's feminine namesake, the Goddess ROMA (whose mystical name spelled backward is the Latin word *amor*; that is, "love").

The names of England's rivers too betray the pervasiveness of an early Goddess religion. All in fact were once ruled by minor but influential goddesses. For example:

- The Goddess BELISAMA ruled the Mersey River.
- The Goddess AERFEN ruled the Dee River.
- The Goddess COVENTINA ("Mother of the [Witches'] Coven") ruled the Carrawburgh River.
- The Goddess SABRINA ruled the Severn River.
- The Goddess CLUTOIDA ruled the Clyde River.
- The Goddess BRIANT ruled the Briant River.
- The Goddess DEVONA ruled the Devon River.
- The Goddess VERBEIA ruled the Wharfe River.
- The Goddess VAGA ruled the Wye River.
- And, as mentioned, BRIGANTIA ruled the Brent River.

Many of these goddesses, such as COVENTINA, or the Celto-British Water-Goddess LATIS, also ruled health, prophecy, inspiration, wells, and springs, which is why the ancients left offerings for them at their sacred sites.

This Pagan custom was passed onto the followers of the Christian version of the Water-Goddess, the VIRGIN MARY, whose very name means "sea water" (the word marine derives from the Latin root of her name: *mare*, "sea"), and one of whose Pagan titles is *Stella Maris* ("Star of the Sea").

And so, like their ancient counterparts, modern followers of Mary's Cult also leave offerings for her at her sacred sites, such as the springs at Lourdes, France.

GODDESS IN SCOTLAND

Ancient England was not an isolated case of religious matricentricity. Indeed, at one time she was surrounded on all sides by cultures, societies, and nations who swore allegiance to both a female Supreme Being and a host of minor goddesses.

Wales (in Welsh, *Cymru*, meaning the "compatriots"), for instance, has an enduring history of Goddess-worship, one dating back to earliest times, as its old Roman name reveals: *Britannus Secunda* ("Britain the Second," or more roughly, the "Second region [after England] devoted to the worship of the Goddess Brigantia").

The Glamorgan (or Gla-Morgan) region of southern Wales takes its name from the fact that it was once the sacred territory of the great Celtic Triple-Goddess MORGAN (from Glamorgan we also get the word glamor, an ancient name for a witch's spell), while the famed hero-poet Taliesin is said to have been born of the Welsh Triple-Goddess CERRIDWEN ("White Sow"), imaged in Celtic myth as a white female pig who devours the bodies of the dead.

The Welsh Sea-Goddess CREIDDYLAD, and her father the Sea-God Llyr, both live on in Shakespeare's play *King Lear*, CREIDDYLAD as "Cordelia" and Lyr as her father, "King Lear," while the Welsh Warrior-Goddess MABB appears in the bard's play, *Romeo and Juliet*, as "Queen Mab."

As we have seen from such examples as the Callanish Standing Stones, Scotland too is firmly rooted in a belief in a feminine Supreme Being, as is patently obvious from the name of both the Scottish nation and her people, the Scoti.

Both names, in fact, derive from the Goddess SCOTIA or SCOTA (the "Tattooed One"), the first and only deity to have ever ruled the entire nation of Scotland, *and* every Scot.

What is more, the area now known as Scotland literally began as a Goddess-worshiping Pagan region, and has never been entirely christianized, especially in the Highlands and in the rural areas. Indeed, each year Paganism continues to grow in popularity all across Scotland.

Likewise, the Hebridian island of Iona (Greek for [Moon] "light") was named after a female deity; in this case, the Grecian Goddess IO (the "Moon"), the white Cow-Goddess whose followers were known as the Ionians (the "devotees of [the Goddess] IO"). In fact, as the word Hebrides (or He-Brides) itself shows, these islands took their name from BRIDE, the Scottish Gaelic name for the Goddess BRIGID.

Similarly, the Scottish island of Skye took its name from the Celto-Teutonic Goddess whose worship was centered there: SKADI, an Amazonian Queen-Goddess known by the Celts as SCATH, SCATHA, or SCATHACH (according to ancient Celtic myth, SCATH'S rival was the Scottish Queen-Goddess AIFE or AOIFE).

One of Scotland's popular national emblems, Saint Andrew's Cross (still very much alive as the white diagonal cross in the American South's Confederate Flag), is also related to a goddess.[21] When the Vikings invaded Scotland in the 9th Century, they brought with them their own national symbol:

---

21. For more on both the Confederate flag and the Southern Confederacy, see my Civil War books listed in the front matter (supra pp. 2-3); in particular see my titles: *Confederate Flag Facts* and *Everything You Were Taught About the Civil War is Wrong, Ask a Southerner!*

the sacred X-shaped "Cross of Woden," or Wotan or Odin (after whom Woden's Day, or Wednesday, was named). Woden was once the Father-God of Scandinavia, and the son of the far more ancient Mother-Goddess FREYA (or FRIGGA).

At first, the Vikings had to impose the Cross of Woden on a reluctant and defeated Scotland. As the centuries passed, however, it gradually came to be accepted, becoming thoroughly imbedded in Scottish tradition.

During Scotland's final conversion to Christianity, it was, of course, necessary to christianize this deeply Pagan symbol. Thus Church mythographers appended it to the figure of Saint Andrew (himself a christianized personification of the ancient Pagan God Pater ("Father"), one of whose titles was *Andros* ("virile man"), transforming the Cross of Woden, the son of the Goddess FREYA, into the "Cross of Saint Andrew."

Alba, Scotland's earliest known name (mentioned by the Carthaginian navigator Himilco in 500 BCE)—and to this day one of the Scottish Gaelic names for Scotland—derives, like England's original name, from the ancient Celtic "White-faced" Moon-Goddess ALBION: *alba* (*albe* in Middle English) is the Middle Latin and Old English feminine word for white (in the Goddess religion, typically a reference to the "white face" of the Moon).

Hence, early Roman invaders called Scotland *Albania*, "the Land of [the Goddess] ALBION," or more literally: "ALBION'S Land." The Scots still refer to themselves and their country (Scotia), in Gaelic, as *Albannaich*: the "people of [the Goddess] ALBION."

Even Scotland's other Latin name, *Caledonia*, derives from a goddess; in this case the great Celtic Black-Queen-Goddess CAILLECH, referred to as the Crone-Goddess MALA LIATH ("Grey Eyebrows") in Cromarty and Ross, as NICNEVIN ("Bone Mother") in Lothian, and in Irish literature as DIGI NO DUINEACH.

In Scottish myth, CAILLECH is the Goddess CARLIN ("Old Woman"), or CAILLEACH BHEUR ("Hag of Winter"); in Irish myth she is the Water Hag-Goddess CALLY BERRY; in British legend she is Leicester's Goddess BLACK ANNIS; and in India she is the aged Crone-Goddess KALI. Enlightened Scots know that *Caledonia* means "the Land Given by KALI."[22]

---

22. For a detailed discussion on the etymology of the Goddess name Kali, see my book *The Caudills: An Etymological, Ethnological, and Genealogical Study*.

According to Tacitus, there were early Goddess-worshiping Scottish tribes who named themselves after this particular deity. One example was the red-headed *Caledonii*, whose name means "Followers of [the Goddess] Cally."

In Spain, where the Dark Goddess CAILLECH was called CALIFIA, she was said to rule over gold and silver; which is why, in 1542, the Spanish explorer Juan Cabrillo named the mineral-rich area now known as California after her.

Later, in 1579, the English explorer Sir Francis Drake also tried, though unsuccessfully, to name California after a goddess. The name he gave it, "New Albion," honored England's ancient Moon-Goddess ALBION.

Scottish legend holds that Scotland's sea captains are sons of the Mermaid-Goddess CEASG (the result of her matings with human males).

The wise old Scottish Crone-Goddess CARLIN (yet another Celtic personification of Kali) survives today as the "wicked witch" of the *Wizard of Oz*, children's fairy tales, and Halloween, whose black cape, pointed hat, and broom stick, are still worn in the U.S. as costumes by millions of children every October 31.

CARLIN has long ruled as the "Spirit of Halloween," one of the world's oldest festivals, also known as Hallowmass or All Hallows, until it was officially adopted by the Christian Church and renamed All Saints Day. But to Pagans, from early times to the present, October 31 has always been, and will always remain, *Samhain*: the "Feast of the Dead."

Samhain, connected to the universal fall harvest festival, is one of the four Pagan Quarter Days: the Fall Equinox (now christianized as Halloween); the Spring Equinox (now christianized as Easter); the Summer Solstice (now christianized as John the Baptist's birthday and Midsummer); and the Winter Solstice (now christianized as Christmas).

For followers of the Old Religion, it is on these "Threshold Days" that the veil (or threshold or portal) between the material world and the spirit world is at its thinnest, allowing easier communication between the living and the dead.

The task of liaising between these two dimensions fell to a special group of Goddess' matriarchal Pagan priestesses, who early patriarchal Christian priests later denigrated by referring to them as *Wicces* ("Witches"), though the word is actually a fitting one.

Wicce (the Old English feminine word for witch) is related to the Old High German words *wizzi* ("knowledge"), *wizzo* ("sage"), and *wih* ("holy"), as well as the Old English words *witan* ("to know"), and *wigle* ("divination"). In other words, these particular non-Christian women were highly educated, knowledgeable, and enlightened, clearly a threat to Catholic authority and hegemony—which is why the Church demonized them.

CARLIN'S familiars (or sacred animals), owls, black cats, and bats, were transformed by the Church into the "scary creatures" of modern Halloween, while Goddess' fairy companions became the "demons" who terrorize children as they go door-to-door "Trick or Treating"; though even this is nothing more than a christianized version of the old Pagan custom of placating the dead—who returned to earth for one night on Samhain—with food and gifts.

GODDESS ACROSS EUROPE

Greece was named after a Mediterranean Triple-Goddess known as the GRAEAE, literally, "the Gray Ones," that is, the Old Crones. Their names were: PEMPHREDO ("Wasp"), ENYO ("Warrior"), and DEINO ("Terrible"), which is why the early Goddess-worshiping Greeks called themselves the *Graeci*, "worshipers of the Crone."

Dactyl, the Greek word for finger, derives from the collective name of ten Greek Goddesses; in this case, the fatherless DACTYLS, who are said to have brought the science of smithcraft to Greece. The ancient Greek tribe, the *Cleonae*, took their name from their beloved female divinity, the Water-Goddess CLEONE.

Rome was named after the Goddess ROMA, while the Latin people were named after the Goddess LAT ("Milk"), as was Malta—a corruption of the island's original name, which was

Ma Lata ("Mother LAT"). The memory of LAT, also known as the Goddess GALA, GALATEA, ELATH or ELAT, is preserved in many other place-names as well, such as Elátia, Greece, and Elat, Indonesia.

The Roman Mountain-Goddess AETNA gave her name to one of Italy's most famous volcanoes, while the island of Crete was named after the Greek Goddess CRETA or CRETE (though the island's most popular deity was the Goddess BRITOMARTIS, "sweet girl").

The Aurora Borealis was named after the Roman Dawn-Goddess AURORA (identical to the Greek Goddess EOS), while the Latin word for war, *bellum*, and the Latin title for military leaders, *Dux Bellorum* ("Leader-Warrior"), both come from the name of the Roman War-Goddess BELLONA.

BELLONA was later known as MAH-BELLONA, after she was combined with the Cappadocian Earth-Goddess MAH—universally referred to as MA or MAR, but known as MARIA in ancient Rome, as MAID MARIAN in Celtic Britain, and as the VIRGIN MARY in Christianity. From the Goddess MA we also derive the word mama.

The city of Venice (like the Venetian people) takes its name from the Love- and Sex-Goddess VENUS, while the city of Athens takes its name from the Greek Virgin-Goddess ATHENE or ATHENA, who won the honor of governing the city in a contest between herself and the Sea-God Poseidon: when a vote was taken, the men, of course, cast their ballots for the male deity, the women for the female deity. The number of women voters exceeded the men by one, and Athena has been ruling the city ever since. Poseidon's name itself, which means "husband of Da," comes from the ancient Greek Earth-Mother Goddess DA.

Our English word faun derives from the Roman Deer-Goddess FAUNA, also known as BONA DEA ("Good Goddess"), a deity whose yearly secret festival (in December) was open only to women (Roman men who dared trespass on these gatherings were arrested, prosecuted, and punished). Our English word discipline comes from the Roman Goddess of hard work and concentration, DISCIPLINA.

Holland was named—as was the Christian underworld, Hell—after the Germanic Goddess HOLLE (that is, "hole") or HEL ("One Who Hides"), both allusions to the female pudenda, while Denmark and the Danish people take their names from the great Celtic Wisdom Triple-Goddess DANA.

Scandinavia was named after the region's Muse-Goddess, SKADI or SKULD. S*cadinauja*, the original spelling of Scandinavia, means "the Land of [the Goddess] Skadi," a deity whose memory is still preserved in many a Swedish town. For example, Skadalungr means "Skadi's [sacred tree] Grove," while Skadave means "Skadi's Temple."

Albania, as we have seen was named after a goddess, in this case the great European Moon-Goddess ALBION or ALBA ("White Moon" or "White Face"). Albania literally means the "Land of the White Goddess." Alba also gave her name to the cities of Alba, Italy, and Albi, France, as well as to Germany's Elbe River.

Untold numbers of famous European cities also bear the ancient stamp of Goddess-worship. Sicily's most famous Goddess, HYBLA, for example, has lent her name to many Sicilian (now Italian) toponyms. Among them are: Megara Hyblaea; Hybla Heraea; Hybla Major; Hybla Minor; Hybla Galeatis; and the Hyblaean Mountains.

The name of the city of Berne means "She-Bear," a Swiss

reference to the Celts' Bear-Goddess DEA ARTIO (whose husband, the Bear-God Art, later emerged in Celtic myth as "King Arthur"), known in Greece as ARTEMIS.

The Helvetii, a Celtic tribe that flourished in western Switzerland in the 1st Century BCE, were devout worshipers of ARTIO, which is why to this day the heraldic symbol of the city of Berne is a female bear.

Many constellations bear the name of some of Europe's great goddesses, such as CASSIOPEIA and her daughter ANDROMEDA, and VIRGO (the "Virgin"). The nine Greek Goddesses of art and inspiration, collectively known as THE MUSE, are also sometimes known as CASTALIDES, in honor of the Greek Well- and Spring-Goddess CASTALIA, whose sacred fountain became their shrine. THE MUSE, of course, gave us the words muse and museum.

The nation of Europe itself is also a "she," for her name comes from a female divinity: the old Mycenaean Moon-Goddess EUROPA (meaning "Broad Face" or "Wide-eyed One," synonyms for the full Moon).

Entire continents, such as Asia (named after the Greek

Goddess ASIA) and Africa (named after the Latin-Mediterranean Goddess AFRA or APHRO-DITE), bear the appellations of goddesses.

Our planet, Earth, is named after a feminine deity; in this case the old Germanic Mother-Goddess HERTHA or AERTHA, known in Scandinavia as FYORGYN or ERDA.

Even the Universe (from the words *uni*, meaning "one" or "whole," and *versus*, from *vertere*, meaning "to turn") itself takes its name from a goddess. According to ancient Etruscan myth, the original great Creatrix and Virgin-Goddess UNI, gave birth to the entire Cosmos, and so it was named after her.

From this goddess we also derive the words *yoni* (Sanskrit for "vulva"), and the name of the month of June, which was named after the Goddess JUNO, a late Roman personification of the Etruscan UNI.

GODDESS IN IRELAND

None of England's neighbors, however, were as Goddess-oriented as Ireland once was, as the sheer number of Ireland's *Bandia* (Old Irish for "Goddesses") reveals.

Like all early peoples, the ancient Irish envisioned the land beneath their feet as feminine, that is, as Mother-Earth. And so one would expect them to name their country after a goddess—which is exactly what they did.

The female deity they chose was ERIU, an ancient European tutelary Earth-Goddess (in Greece she was called HERA, that is, the "protectress") who forms one-third of an old all-female Irish and Druidic Trinity.

The other two goddesses of this triad are FOLTA and BANBA ("land unplowed for a year"; she was known on the Continent of Europe as CATHUBODIA). One of Ireland's ancient names was "the island of Banba of the Women."

In Irish Gaelic, the phrase "land of ERIU" is written *Erinn* or *Erin* (and is sometimes thought of as a poetic or literary form meaning "from the island to the west"). Modern Irish, however, refer to Ireland as Éire, a word meaning "the Lady ERIU." Over time, ERIU'S Land, that is ÉIRE'S Land, became the word Ireland.

As in England, the names of many of Ireland's rivers also show vestiges of a once thriving Goddess religion. The River Shannon was named after the Goddess SINEND (or SINANN); the River Boyne after the Goddess BOAND (or BOANN); the River Lagan after the Goddess LOGIA; and the River Bride after the Goddess BRIGID, a deity often venerated at wells, hence her alternate name TOBAR BRIDE (literally "Well Bride")—a divinity identical to the Fire-Goddess of County Donegal, AIBHEAOG.

The Cliffs of Moher still retain many of the names of the goddesses who have long ruled them: the Goddess BRONACH (identical to CAILLEACH, who is also known in Ireland as CAILAINN) governs the Burren nearby, while the cliff known as "Hag's Head" takes its name from the Goddess CEANN CAILIGHE; the cliff called "the Hag of Black Head" is named after the Goddess CAILEACH CINN BOIRNE. The Irish Swan-

Goddess CAER ("Yew Berry") is said to still live on the lake of the Dragon's Mouth.

Irish cities and islands also bear the matronymic imprint of an early period of Goddess-worship. Miltown Malbay, for instance, was named after the Celtic Goddess MAL. And Dublin (in Old Irish, *Aith Cliath*; in Modern Irish, *Duibhlinn*; in Old Norse, *Dyflin*; in Anglo-Norman, *Dublinne*), as another example, takes its name from the old Celtic Sea-Goddess DUBH LACHA ("Black Lake," "Dark Water," or "Dark Pool").

Achill Island, Achill Head, and the town of Achill, were all named after the Celtic Goddess ACHALL, while Beare Island, in Bantry Bay, continues to be ruled over by the ancient Celtic Sun- and Horse-Goddess ETAIN ("Swift One").

Western Ireland's famous mountain range, Slieve Aughty (in Irish Gaelic, *Sliabh na Echtghe*), was named after the country's pre-Celtic Mother-Goddess ECHTGHE or AUGHTY. The WHITE WITCH OF CLARE (or BIDDY EARLY) is still said to dwell in the region of Feakle Parish nearby.

County Tipperary's "Twelve Mountains of Ebhlinne" belong to the Irish Mother-Mountain-Goddess EBHLINNE, after whom they were named. To this day, the tallest of these twelve hills is called *Mathair-Shliabh*, meaning "Mother Mountain."

Ireland's Bay of Aige was named after the Irish Deer-Goddess AIGE, while in southern Ireland the Hill of Almha takes its name from the ancient Irish Goddess ALMHA or ALMU.

The Coll Buana, a hazel tree, was named after the Irish Seer-Goddess BUAN, while the canola grain (also known as rape seed) takes its name from the Celtic Goddess CANOLA, who invented the Irish harp.

The Irish Bird-Goddess CLIODNA or CLIDNA ("Shapely One"), gave her name to the hill in Cork known as *Carrig Cliodna*, and because she takes the form of every ninth swell upon the sea, large waves are still sometimes referred to as "CLIDNA'S Waves."

Certainly two of the most celebrated Irish Goddess sites are the twin peaks of County Kerry, the Goddess mountains known as the Paps of Anu (literally "the Breasts of Anu"), named after the great ancestral Irish Wisdom- and Triple-Goddess ANU, DANA, DANE, DANU, or (in Welsh) DON, the "Mother of All Deities" (according to ancient Celtic legend the

Irish Fairy-Queen CRED, or CREIDE, dwells in the Paps of Anu). Hills and mountains have long been archetypal symbols of the Earth-Mother's milk-giving breasts, pregnant womb, and life-giving *Mons Veneris* ("Mountain of Venus").

DANA'S name comes from the Old Celtic word *dan*, meaning "knowledge" (the first Christians, the Gnostics, knew DANA as SOPHIA, "wisdom"). She not only gave her name to many Old World rivers—such as the Danube, the Don, the Dnieper, and the Dniestr—but also, as we have seen, to Denmark and her people (the Danes) as well.

The antiquity of this truly ancient female deity can be seen in the fact that she was worshiped thousands of years ago among the pre-Hellenic Aegeans, where she was known as DANUNA. To the early Greeks she was DANAE, while in Russian myth she is called DENNITSA.

In Sumeria and Babylon, where she was known as DAM-KINA and DUNNU respectively, DANA was venerated as a Virgin-Earth-Goddess who gave birth to the divine Savior-Son.

In Scandinavia legend DANA is the wise and judgmental Crone-Goddess ANGURBODA, the "Hag of the Iron Wood," while the ancient Hebrews knew her as DINAH ("justified" or "judged"). The members of one biblical tribe were such devout followers of her that they named themselves after her: the Danites.[23]

The Germanic Saxons called this Goddess DANU-ANA. To the Angles she was ANNA. After these two German tribes invaded the British Isles, they came to know her as the BLUE HAG, BLACK ANNIS, CAT ANA, GENTLE ANNIE, or BLACK AGNES. The Goddess' ancient English cave-shrine in Leicestershire, still revealingly known as "DANE's Hill," was originally called "BLACK ANNIS' Bower."

The ubiquitousness of DANA's presence in early Irish life is at once overt and incontrovertible: according to the Celtic creed, the Irish people trace their ancestry directly back to DANA'S followers, a Bronze Age tribe known as the *Tuatha De Danann*, meaning "the People of the Goddess DANA." Later, under the anti-female sentiments of the early orthodox Christian Church (that is, Catholicism), DANA'S followers were reduced to mere nature spirits, the legendary *Daoine Sidhe*; that is, "Dana's Fairies."

The entire Celtic race was believed to have been civilized by

---

23. Judges 18:30.

a goddess; in this case a female divinity known as BASILEA, whose name derives from the Greek word basile, "queen," the title of numerous ancient goddesses. BASILEA gave us the word basilica, an early type of Christian church design.

At this point it should come as no surprise to learn that Ireland's patron saint (Saint Patrick), Ireland's national holiday (Saint Patrick's Day), and one of Ireland's national symbols (the shamrock), all have their origins in Celtic Goddess-worship.

In ancient Ireland March 17 marked DANA'S annual "Green Day," the Triple-Goddess' holy day of spring rebirth (many other Mother-Earth-Goddesses also rule the Spring, such as DEMETER, one of whose names is CHLOË, meaning "Green"). At this time DANA was inseminated by her male consort, the Celtic Shamrock-God, a triune deity called *Trefuilngid Tre-Eochair*, whose name means the "Triple-Bearer of the Triple-Key." The phrase "triple-key" here is a euphemism for the three-lobed shamrock, or trefoil, a symbol of the Triple-God's triple-phallus.

Under the Christian Faith Trefuilngid Tre-Eochair—the ever-begetting Father-God—was eventually transformed into "Saint

Patrick," a Christian character who himself (like "Saint Andrew") was built upon the figure of the old Roman gate-keeping, key-bearing phallic rock-god, *Petra* ("Rock") or *Pater Patrum* ("Father of Fathers"), who guarded the gates of the Great Triple-Goddess' temples across the ancient Graeco-Roman world.

New Testament mythographers transformed the Pagan *Pater* into the Christian *Petros* or "Saint 'Peter'" (his name later became corrupted to papa, then pope), who symbolized the Christian key-holding, rock-god upon which the Church was to be built.[24] (This view, however, was later rejected by the Gnostically oriented Saint Paul, who saw Christ, not Peter, as "the Rock.")[25]

During this christianization process, the triple-phallus symbol, the shamrock, was appended to the figure of Saint Patrick, at which time it also became a symbol of the all-male Holy Trinity, "the Father, the Son, and the Holy Spirit."

This assimilation, however, cannot obfuscate another truth embedded in ancient Celtic Goddess-worship. The feminine

---

24. Matthew 16:18-19.
25. 1 Corinthians 10:4.

symbolism of the shamrock predates the innovation of male religion by thousands of years; for in Ireland, it originally represented the world's first Holy Trinity, the all-female Triple-Goddess DANA, comprised of the Maiden, the Mother, and the Crone—divine personifications of earthly birth, life, and death; or the mind-body-spirit complex.

The Celts and the Goddess Kelle

The Celts (or Kelts) themselves derive their name from a great Celtic female deity, in this case the Mother-Goddess KELLE (hence this people was called the *Keltoi* by the Greeks and the *Celtai* by the Romans), known among Hindus as KALI, whose name means "cave" or "dark hole," another reference to the vulvaic entrance to the magical female womb "from whence all life springs."

The Pagan KELLE—later christianized as the counterfeit "Saint Kilda"—had shrines on her sacred island, KELLE'S Island (now known as "Saint Kilda's Isle"), and at Kildare, a city named after KELLE'S priestesses, the *Kele-De*, meaning "the Spirit of the Goddess KELLE" (the Irish word *kill*, meaning a dark room or "cell," or "cave," once denoted one of KELLE'S shrines). Those with the surname Kelly (or its many variations, Kelley, Kellie, MacKelly, McKelly, O'Kelly, etc.) can claim tribal descent from this goddess.[26]

Modern Gaels (like the words Gaelic and Gallic) can trace their etymological origins back to the ancient Moon-Goddess of Paphos called GALATEIA ("milky white"), or GALA-TEA or GA-LAT-EA, that is, the "Milk-Goddess." The ancient Celtic tribes who lived in what is now Turkey held that they were descended from this same goddess, whom they knew as GALA (Greek for "Mother's Milk") or QUEEN GALATA.

Quite naturally they took her name, not only calling themselves the Gauls, but naming their territory after her, Galatia: "Land of [the Goddess] GALA." The New Testament book of *Galatians* reveals Paul's frustration at not being able to convert the stubborn Goddess-worshiping Celts he met there.

QUEEN GALA'S male consort, Sir Galahad, too was named after her, as is Gaeldom itself (in Scottish Gaelic, *Gaidhealtachd*).

Not only do the words lactic and lactation come from the name of the Celtic Milk-Goddess GALA, so does the name of the vast cosmic wheel that our planet resides in.

---

[26]. Additional material on the topic of Kelle specifically (as well as the subject of thealogy generally) may be found in my work, *The Book of Kelle: An Introduction to Goddess-Worship and the Great Celtic Mother-Goddess Kelle, Original Blessed Lady of Ireland*.

The ancients believed that the meandering stream-like band of stars across the night sky was Goddess' breast-milk. Hence, they called it *Galaxias* or *Galakt* (in English, galaxy); that is, the Goddess' "Milky Way."

Centuries later, early Celtic Britons worshiped the milky white Moon-Goddess GALA as ALBION, and, as we have seen, named their nation after her.

The connection between Gaelic culture, the word galaxy, and the Goddess GALA can also be seen in the proper pronunciation of the word Gaelic: GAL-lick, as in GAL-axy, not GAY-lick, as is commonly assumed.

11

The Cow-Goddesses

Goddess, in her form as a milk-giving Lunar deity, was often portrayed as a cow, a maternal bovine symbol known as the "Mother of the Stars," which is why the ancient Celts called the Milky Way *Bothar-bó-finné*, or "Track of the White Cow."

The ancient British Isles were home to countless Cow-Goddesses, such as Celtic Ireland's White-Cow-Fertility-Goddess BOUVINDA; the White-Cow-Goddess BO FIND; the Red-Cow-Goddess BO RUADH; the Black-Cow-Goddess BO DHU; the Blue-Cow-Goddess GLAS; and BOANN ("She of the White Cows"), the Cow-Goddess who gave her name to, and who still rules, the River Boyne.

Numerous place-names recall the memory of Ireland's feminine bovine deities, such as, LOUGH-NA-BO ("Cow's Lake") and TOBER-BO-FINN ("Well of the White Cow"). Irish legend states that all the cows of Ireland descend from the Cow-Goddess BO FIND.

Many other ancient nations possessed Moon-Cow-Goddesses as well; for example, Egypt (the Goddess HATHOR), Greece (the Goddess HERA), Israel (the Goddess ASHERAH), Sumeria (the Goddess ASTARTE and the Goddess AMASHILAMMA), and Scandinavia (the Goddess AUDHUMBLA). Their udders were said to pour forth "star-milk that nourishes all life," lactic liquid whose curds these Creatrix-Goddesses used to form stars, moons, planets, and living beings.

Modern English culture retains the tradition of the old Celtic Moon-Cow-Goddess in her nursery rhymes as "the cow that jumped over the Moon," and in the old wive's tale which states that "the Moon is made of cheese." Many such legends grew up around these female deities, as well as many others, like Ireland's Cattle-Goddess DIL.

12

SAINT BRIDGET AND THE VIRGIN MARY

Contrary to what is traditionally taught, British Goddess worship did not die with the arrival of Christianity on England's shores. In fact, the Church unknowingly helped resuscitate and promote it.

When the early Christian Fathers found that they could not eradicate either Goddess religion or the Goddess BRIGANTIA from the British Isles, they simply adopted and "converted" her, creating the fictional figure of "Saint Bride" or "Saint Bridget," nicknamed "Biddy."

In her new guise as a Christian saint, BRIGANTIA'S status was demoted, becoming a mere servant—under the title *Ban-Chuideachaidh Moire* ("Aid-Woman")—of the VIRGIN MARY; though other myths asserted that she was baptized by Saint Patrick (an impossibility since he lived some 400 years after

Mary).

Despite the efforts of the Church, her transformation can scarcely conceal Saint Bridget's origins as BRIGANTIA, for the Christian mythographers who created the bogus saint appended all of the Goddess' traits to her, creating little more than a perfect christianized replica of the great Pagan Goddess of England.

For example,

- BRIGANTIA rules smithcraft; Saint Bridget's priests are goldsmiths.

- BRIGANTIA governs the muse; Saint Bridget is called upon for creative inspiration.

- BRIGANTIA is waited upon by priestesses; Saint Bridget is waited upon by nuns.

- BRIGANTIA is served by priests; Saint Bridget is served by bishops.

- BRIGANTIA oversees medicine; Saint Bridget is called upon

in prayers for healing.

Thus it is that Britain's greatest and most popular deity continues to be honored and invoked, though unknowingly, by millions of devout Christian Britons.

So deeply rooted is the Goddess BRIGANTIA in the collective Celtic unconscious that in Ireland Saint Bridget is even more popular than the VIRGIN MARY, who is herself a Christian version of a Pagan female deity.

The figure of the VIRGIN MARY was patterned on the great universal Mother-Goddess MA (Mama) or MAR, known in Syria as MARI; in Greece as MYRRHA; in Rome as MARIA; in Egypt as MERI; in Babylonia as MARRATU; in Israel as MARAH; in India as KEL-MARI; in Buddhism as MARA; in Scandinavia as MAERIN; and later in Anglo-Celtic mythology as MAID MARIAN. As its name indicates, the 5,000 year-old Amorite city of Mari (on the modern Syrian-Iraqi border) was once the center of Mari's worship.

The Amorites also knew MARI, though by the name AMOR ("love"), and so named themselves after her. In ancient Italy, where her name was occultly spelled backwards, ROMA, she gave her name to the Romans and their Empire.

According to Hebrew scholars, the Amorites—also known as the Martu—were the original ancestors of the Jews;[27] and so it is not surprising to learn, as the Bible clearly states, that the Jews themselves were also once a matriarchal people who venerated a female Supreme Being, an all-powerful "Queen of Heaven" they called ASHERAH ("Straight").

ASHTORETH, as she was also known, was the female consort of the Hebrew Father-God Yahweh-Jehovah-Jove-Jupiter,[28] a male deity whose very name derives from a goddess; in this case, the ancient Hebrew Goddess IAHU ANAT.

The Goddess IAHU was masculinized by early patriarchal Hebrew priests, who transformed her into the male deity Jahi or Yahweh, who himself is identical in name and character to both the Greek Father-God Zeus (from the Sanskrit *Dyaus Pitar*, "Heavenly Father") and the Roman Father-God Jupiter (from *Iu-Pater*, "the Father"), also known as Jove ("The Youth").

---

27. Genesis 10:16; 14:7; 15:16; 48:22.
28. 1 Kings 11:33.

Another example of a well-known male deity who, some say, began life as a goddess is the Arabian Father-God Allah (the "God"). A number of religious scholars maintain that he is a masculinized version of the far more ancient Arabian female deity ALLAT or AL-LAT (the "Goddess"), while traditionalists assert that she was a daughter of Allah, and therefore could not be either older than he or his female equivalent. What we do know is that AL-LAT is identical to the Near-Eastern Goddess LAT, who was known as LATONA ("Queen Goddess") in Rome and as LETO ("Darkness") in ancient Greece.[29]

According to Arabian mythology AL-LAT is one of the three goddesses who, along with the Crone-Goddess AL-UZZA ("the Mighty"), and the Virgin-Goddess Q'RE ("Heart"), comprises matriarchal Arabia's original all-female Trinity, known as MENAT or MANAT, the "Threefold Moon."

In the ancient world, the most popular of these three figures was the Virgin-Goddess Q'RE, also known as KORE ("Maiden") among whose followers was a group called the Koreshites (that is, Kore-Shites). She was also known as KHER, KER, CARA, CARNA, CERES, CORE, KAUR, and KAULI, though all of these

---

29. Whatever one's beliefs concerning Allah, it is clear that he is the same Great Father, widely known simply as "God," who has been and continues to be worshiped by Jews, Muslims, Christians, and Pagans. Saint Paul himself noted this fact some 2,000 years ago (see, e.g., Acts 17:22-23).

are merely variations of the name of the Goddess KALI, known in the British Isles, as we have seen, as KELLE ("Cave")—whose enormous temples in Brittany, France, date back some 5,000 years.

From KORE, the archetypal "Holy Virgin" of pre-Christian Greece, we derive the words core, carnage, carnitine, carnival, cereal, cardiac, carnivore, carnivorous, corn, kernel, carnation, and carnal. Mount Carmel was named after her as well, as this site was once one of KORE'S most important shrines in Israel. KORE'S name became the literal word for "heart" in many languages, such as Latin (*cor*), French (*coeur*), Greek (*kardia*), Spanish (*corazón*), Portuguese (*coração*), and Italian (*cuore*).

The number five has long been associated with mother-goddesses, for the outstretched human body, a symbol of life, has five points (the head, two hands, and two feet). Since the apple reveals a five-pointed star, or pentacle (a symbol of the Soul), when cut in half, and the apple blossom has five petals, the apple was seen as KORE'S sacred fruit, which is why an apple's "heart" is to this day still referred to as a core.

In Rome, where KORE was known as CARNA, her annual

festival was called the *Carnival*, the origin of our modern English word of the same spelling. In ancient Egypt KORE'S festival, celebrated on January 6, was called the Koreion. Later, patriarchal Christianity, in a vain attempt to rid the world of Goddess-worship, adopted this Pagan festival and renamed it the "Feast of Epiphany."

In Christian Britain the Koreion was transformed into the "Feast of Our Lady of Mercy" (originally known there as "Kirn," or the "Feast of Ingathering"). But this Christian-created mythic fog cannot conceal the fact that the original "Virgin" here was the Pagan Virgin-Goddess KORE, the third member of AL-LAT'S all-female Holy Trinity.

At AL-LAT'S shrine in Mecca, she was venerated in the form of a great black stone, called the Ka'abe or Kubaba ("Cube"), a word derived from the name of another notable female divinity, the Phrygian Mother-Goddess, CYBELE, "the Most Holy One"—whose temple in Rome was the original site on which Saint Peter's Basilica now stands. (In Phoenicia, CYBELE was known as BA'ALAT, BAALTIS, or BELILI, "Lady," the wife of the God Baal, whose name means "Lord.")

Some say that the Shi'ites, a sect of Islam, trace their descent from Fatima, the daughter of Mohammed. From a scholarly, poetic, or mythological point of view, Fatima would merely be another personification of AL-LAT, as her name reveals: FATIMA means "the Creatress," one more title of the great Mother-Goddess, two of whose sacred emblems, the Lunar Crescent and the five-pointed Pentacle (or Star), can still be seen in Islam's sacred symbol: ☪

Star-Goddesses, from ASTARTE ("Womb") and ISHTAR ("Star") to DIANA-LUCIFERA ("Queen of Heaven"-"Bringer of Light") and VENUS ("Sexual Love"), are abundant in the world's religions, including Christianity. Here, the VIRGIN MARY is today still referred to under her pre-Christian Pagan title *Stella Maris* ("Star of the Sea"), and is tellingly depicted in the book of Revelation just like her Pagan predecessors: standing on a crescent Moon, wearing a crown of twelve stars (symbolizing the twelve star-signs of the astrological Zodiac).[30]

ASTARTE, ISHTAR, DIANA-LUCIFERA, and VENUS, all who possessed the title the "Morning Star" (due to their connection with the planet Venus), served, in fact, as prototypes for the VIRGIN MARY, whose divine Sun/Son-God, Jesus, like the Devil ("slanderer")—who is also known as Satan ("adversary")

---

30. Revelation 12:1.

or Lucifer ("Bringer of Light")—was also called the "Morning Star" by biblical authors.[31]

After the Patriarchal Takeover in Arabia, the religion of Islam emerged, and with it AL-LAT disappeared. With AL-LAT'S obliteration, her sacred black Yoni stone, the Ka'abe ("Cube") was taken over by the new Islamic patriarchs, and today remains the center of Islamic worship.

Still, as many religious scholars have noted, Arabic myth itself seems to suggest that Allah was once connected to the great Arabian Mother-Goddess AL-LAT in some manner. For as we have seen, Allah is identical to the Jewish Father-God Yahweh (known in Christianity as Jehovah), whose wife was the great Hebrew Mother-Goddess ASHERAH, who is identical to AL-LAT.

"Lady ASHERAH of the Sea," like so many goddesses, was known by many names in the ancient world. To the Egyptians she was ASHESH or AU SET (that is, ISIS, who gave her name to one-third of the word Israel)[32]; to the Sumerians ASHNAN or

---

31. Revelation 22:16; Isaiah 14:12; 2 Corinthians 11:14.
32. The word Israel derives from the names of three deities, one female, two males: Isis-Ra-El. Headed by the Egyptian Goddess Isis (mother of the Divine Son-God Horus), on whom the Virgin Mary was closely modeled, Isis-Ra-El was an ancient Semitic Trinity.

ASTARTE; to the Anatolians ANATH; to the Ugarites as ANAT; to the Arabs ATHTAR; to the Hurrians ATTART; and by the Babylonians as ISHTAR ("Star").[33]

Hebrew women were still performing the annual ritual of mourning over the sacrificial death of ASHERAH'S virgin-born Solar-Savior-Son-God, Tammuz (one of the many pre-Christian prototypes used in the paganization of Jesus), at the gate of the Jewish Temple as late as the 4th Century BCE.[34]

Indeed, from the beginning, Hebrew women were far more enthusiastic about Goddess-worship than most Hebrew men (King Solomon being the best known exception to this),[35] which is why they wore Moon pendants in her honor,[36] and passed a belief in ASHERAH down from mother to daughter.

The Hebrew Queen Maacah and her daughter Jezebel, for example, openly worshiped ASHERAH in her sacred tree groves, a practice for which the former was deposed,[37] and the latter was cruelly murdered by patriarchal Hebrew priests.[38] Jezebel's daughter, the Hebrew Queen Athaliah, also tried to

---

33. See 1 Kings 11:5; 31-33; Jeremiah 7:18; 44:15-25.
34. Ezekiel 8:14.
35. 1 Kings 11:5.
36. Isaiah 3:17-18.
37. 1 Kings 15:10-13.
38. 2 Kings 10:29-37.

revive Goddess-worship among her people, a deed for which she received the same fate as Jezebel.[39]

Suffering from what the Austrian psychiatrist Sigmund Freud would later call the "Whore-Madonna Complex" (in which women are seen as either aggressive sexual predators or as passive asexual virgins), 2nd- and 3rd-Century Jews and Jewish-Christians saw this ubiquitous female Supreme Being—whose Pagan image and religion is known to have existed in nearly every ancient society, under thousands of different names—as a highly dualistic figure.

On the one hand they demonized ASHERAH, calling her "the Great Whore of Babylon."[40] On the other hand they adopted and christianized her, merging her into the figure of their own great Virgin-Goddess, MA/MAR/MARI/MARIAM/MERI/MARY (mother of the sacrificial Solar-Savior Son-God, Jesus), a female deity still known by modern Christians under ASHERAH'S old Pagan-Jewish title, the "Queen of Heaven."[41]

The profound role that MARI (in the British Isles, known as BRIGID, BRIGANTIA, or BRITANNIA) once played in shaping

---

39. 2 Kings 11:20.
40. Revelation 17:5.
41. Jeremiah 7:18; 44:19.

Western culture can be seen in the fact that from her we derive the word marriage.

In ancient Rome couples were encouraged to wed "in the name of MARI," a goddess known there as MARIA. This ceremony, referred to in Latin as *Maritare* (that is, *Mari-Tare*), literally means "union under the auspices of [the Goddess] MARI."

Over the centuries the word *Maritare*, adopted by England via France—from the Old French word *marier* ("to marry")—became anglicized, forming our modern English word marriage ("the state, or process, of being married").

Whatever one chooses to call this goddess, MARI, MARIA, MARIAN, or MARY, she is without question the single most popular deity on earth today. In Christianity alone, for example, of the world's 1 billion Catholics, most pray to MARY rather than to Jesus. As a result, the majority of Catholic Churches display a statue of Mary rather than Jesus outside their front doors.

MARY'S connections with the Pagan Goddess BRIGANTIA are never far away. The Church not only made BRIGANTIA (as

"Saint Bridget") the servant of MARY, but it also installed her as the foster mother of MARY'S son, Jesus, which is why Saint Bridget is still sometimes referred to as *Muime Chriosda* ("Foster Mother of Christ").

100 ~ BRITANNIA RULES

13

Ancient Remnants of Goddess-Worship in Modern England

There are other more overt signs of contemporary British Goddess-worship, however, a feminine spirituality that continues to permeate every aspect of modern Anglo-Celtic life. We have, for instance:

🐍 Anglo-Celtic Goddess *politics*, such as the British love of queens and the superior role of the Queen of England compared to that of her subordinate husband (who is often seen as little more than her consort).

🐍 Anglo-Celtic Goddess *customs*, such as well dressings, the wearing of the Green, the hanging of horseshoes, and the idea of "ladies first."

🕮 Anglo-Celtic Goddess *rituals*, many now christianized, such as the Agape, baptism, blessing, prayer, meditation, the Eucharist, and the Rosary.

🕮 Anglo-Celtic Goddess *holy days*, many now christianized, such as Candlemas, Christmas, Easter, Halloween, Lammas, Lent, May Eve and May Day, Midsummer, Mothering Sunday (Mother's Day in the U.S.), New Year, and the Sabbath.

🕮 Anglo-Celtic Goddess *symbols*, such as the Celtic Cross—an ancient sacred emblem of the sexual-spiritual union of the Female Principle (the Lunar circle) mystically penetrated by the Male Principle (the Solar cross): ☘

We also have:

🕮 Anglo-Celtic Goddess *statuary*, such as the SHEILA NA GIG, a Celtic Life-and-Death-Goddess still displayed in the United Kingdom's church architecture as an "obscene gargoyle."

🕮 Anglo-Celtic *place-names*, such as Bridewell (that is, "BRIGANTIA'S Well"), a district in London that once served as a holy spring-shrine devoted to the Celto-British Goddess BRIGANTIA).

Anglo-Celtic Goddess *myths*, such as those surrounding the BANSHEE, LADY GUINEVERE, MAID MARIAN, and LADY GODIVA.

England's national flower, the rose—long a mystical vulva symbol of female deities worldwide, is itself an overt reminder of an age when Goddess, not God, ruled this land.

And let us not forget that today there are thousands of modern British Neopagans (Goddess-worshipers), women and men who count themselves as her devotees (a number that is growing each year), and who wear the triple spiral in her honor.

Wicce (Witchcraft, or simply the Craft) and Druidry, both vestigial branches of the Old Religion (that is, Goddess-worship), are more popular than ever across the British Isles (the names of the Anglo-Celtic goddesses that were, and which continue to be, venerated by European Wiccens and Druids number in the thousands), and the old Gaelic salutation, *Bithidh a'bhandia leat* ("Goddess be with you"), is once again being heard across the land.

14

BRITANNIA RULES

While most modern Britons and Celts have ousted their eponymous Goddesses (that is, BRITANNIA and KELLE) from their thrones and replaced them with a male Father-God, it can still truly be said that "BRITANNIA rules," and that she always will.

Not on political, conscious, and religious levels (as our male Father-God does), but rather on psychological, unconscious, and spiritual ones—deep in the hearts and souls of the citizens of a nation that should rightfully be called, not the United Kingdom, but the United Queendom.

Even ignoring the vast archaeological evidence, it is more than apparent from etymology, place-names, cultural traditions, social customs, and myth alone, that the roots of Anglo-Celtic culture are firmly implanted in the soil of the world's oldest sacred tradition: Goddess-worship.

15

GODDESS-OGRAPHY

As further evidence that the British Isles evolved over thousands of years in the crucible of Goddess-worship, I offer the following list.

In it we find chronicled just a few of the countless major and minor female deities that have been venerated, followed, honored, and loved by millions of people throughout England, Wales, Scotland, Ireland, Brittany, Cornwall, Galacia, and the Isle of Man over the past few millennia.

The 257 divinities listed here represent a tiny fraction of the total female pantheon of the early Anglo-Celtic people. As archaeologists dig through their fossil remains, evidence of new, heretofore unknown goddesses continue to surface on an almost daily basis.[42]

---

[42]. These are discovered mainly through ancient inscriptions.

Many of these goddesses not only sustain large groups of believers right into the present day, but also continue to draw new followers throughout the British Isles (and elsewhere).

These names stand as defiant emblems against the doubting Thomases of science and patriarchal religion; each one a bold and overt testament of the Celtic-British love of female religion (thealogy) and its Supreme Being, Goddess.

257 Goddesses of the British Isles

A partial list

Note: While some of the goddesses listed here were neither British or Celtic, they were worshiped by early British and Celtic peoples and so are included.

Abnoba	Aerten
Achall	Aeval
Achtan	Agrona
Acionna	Aibheaog
Actland	Aife
Adsullata	Aige
Aeracura	Ailinn
Aerfen	Aimend
Aeron	Ain

Aine	Bandonga
Airmed	Bandua
Alaisiagae	Banshee
Almha	Basilea
Ancamma	Beag
Ancasta	Bean Nighe
Andarta	Bebhionn
Andraste	Bé Chuille
Anne	Becuma
Annea Clivana	Belisima
Anu	Benvarry
Aoibhell	Berecyntia
Ardwina	Bergusia
Argante	Biddy
Ariadne	Biddy Mannion
Arianrhod	Black Annis
Arnamentia	Blathnat
Artio	Blodewedd
Aufaniae	Bo Find
Aveta	Boann
Badb	Bormana
Ban Naomha	Branwen
Banba	Bri
Ban-Chuideachaidh Moire	Bricta

Bride
Brigantia
Brigid
Britannia
Bronach
Buan
Caer
Cailleach
Caireen
Cally Berry
Campestres
Camma
Canola
Caolainn
Carlin
Carman
Carravogue
Cartimandua
Cathubodia
Ceasg
Ceibhfhionn
Cerridwen
Cessair
Cethlion

Cetnenn
Chlaus Haistic
Clidna
Clota
Cocidius
Condwiramur
Corchen
Corra
Coventia
Cred
Creiddylad
Crobdh Dearg
Cyhiraeth
Cymidei Cymeinfoll
Dahut
Damara
Dames Vertes
Damona
Da
Danu
Dea Nutrix
Deae Matres
Dechtere
Deirdre

Devorgilla	Ethne
Dia Griene	Fachea
Dil	Fand
Divona	Feithline
Domnu	Fideal
Don	Finchoem
Druantia	Findabar
Dubh Lacha	Finncaev
Eadon	Fiongalla
Ebhlinne	Fionnuala
Echtghe	Fithir
Edain	Flidais
Ele	Fotla
Emer	Gaillimh inion Breasail
Eostre	Gallia
Epona	Gentle Annie
Erce	Gillagriene
Erecura	Glas
Eri of the Golden Hair	Godiva
Eriu	Goewin
Ernmas	Góntia
Ess Euchen	Grainne
Estiu	Grainne ni Malley
Etain	Grian

Guinevere
Gwyar
Gwyllion
Habetrot
Habondia
Henwen
Ianuaria
Icovellauna
Inciona
Inghean Bhuidhe
Iouga
Korrigan
Latiaran
Latis
Lavercam
Leanan Sidhe
Le Fay
Liban
Litavis
Logia
Luaths Lurgann
Mabb
Macha
Maeve

Magog
Mal
Mala Liath
Marcia Proba
Mari
Matres
Medb
Melusine
Minerva Medica
Modron
Momu
Moncha
Mongfind
Morgan Le Fay
Morgay
Moriath
Mor Muman
Morrigan
Moruadh
Muime Chriosda
Muireartach
Munanna
Nanna
Nantosuelta

Nar	Scotia
Naria	Senuna
Nehalennia	Sequana
Nemain	Sheila na Gig
Nemetona	Silkie
Nessa	Sin
Niamh	Sinann
Nicnevin	Sirona
Nimue	Souconna
Oanuava	Sulis
Odras	Suliviae
Olwen	Taillte
Oona	Tamesis
Penarddun	Telo
Ratis	Tlachtga
Rhiannon	Triduana
Ricagumbeda	Turrean
Ritona	Uairebhuidhe
Rosmerta	Varia
Saba	Veleda
Sabrina	Verbeia
Satiada	Viviane
Scathach	Xusigiae
Scota	

"Ye are gods."

JESUS

(John 10:34)

BIBLIOGRAPHY

Adler, Margot. *Drawing Down the Moon.* Boston, MA: Beacon Press, 1981.

Agha-Jaffar, Tamara. *Women and Goddesses in Myth and Sacred Text.* New York, NY: Longman, 2004.

Albright, William Powell. *Yahweh and the Gods of Canaan.* New York, NY: Doubleday, 1968.

Allen, Paula Gunn. *The Sacred Hoop: Recovering the Feminine in American Indian Traditions.* Boston, MA: Beacon Press, 1986.

Allison, Dale C., Jr. *Resurrecting Jesus: The Earliest Christian Tradition and Its Interpreters.* New York, NY: T and T Clark, 2005.

Andrews, Ted. *The Occult Christ: Angelic Mysteries, Seasonal Rituals, and the Divine Feminine.* St. Paul, MN: Llewellyn, 1993.

Angus, Samuel. *The Mystery-Religions and Christianity: A Study of the Religious Background of Early Christianity.* 1925. New York, NY: Citadel Press, 1966 ed.

Ardrey, Robert. *African Genesis.* 1961. New York, NY: Dell, 1972 ed.

———. *The Territorial Imperative.* 1966. New York, NY: Delta, 1968 ed.

Armstrong, Herbert W., Keith W. Stump, and John Halford. *The Plain Truth About Christmas.* 1952. Pasadena, CA: Worldwide Church of God, 1986 ed.

Armstrong, Karen. *A History of God: The 4000-Year Quest of Judaism, Christianity and Islam.* New York, NY: Knopf, 1993.

Ashe, Geoffrey. *The Virgin: Mary's Cult and the Re-emergence of the Goddess.* 1976. London, UK: Arkana, 1988 ed.

———. *Dawn Behind the Dawn: A Search for the Earthly Paradise.* New York, NY: Henry Holt, 1992.

Atkins, Gaius Glenn, and Charles Samuel Braden. *Procession of the*

Gods. 1930. New York, NY: Harper and Brothers Publishers, 1936 ed.

Attwater, Donald. *The Penguin Dictionary of Saints*. 1965. Harmondsworth, UK: Penguin, 1983 ed.

Avalon, Arthur. *Shakti and Shakta*. New York, NY: Dover, 1978.

Ayto, John. *Dictionary of Word Origins*. New York, NY: Arcade, 1990.

Bachofen, Johann Jakob. *Myth, Religion and Mother Right*. Princeton, NJ: Princeton University Press, 1967.

Baigent, Michael. *The Jesus Papers: Exposing the Greatest Cover-Up in History*. San Francisco, CA: Harper San Francisco, 2006.

Baigent, Michael, and Richard Leigh. *The Dead Sea Scrolls Deception*. 1991. New York, NY: Touchstone, 1993 ed.

Baigent, Michael, Richard Leigh, and Henry Lincoln. *Holy Blood, Holy Grail*. 1982. New York, NY: Dell, 1983. ed.

——. *The Messianic Legacy*. New York, NY: Dell, 1986.

Baring, Anne, and Jules Cashford. *The Myth of the Goddess: Evolution of an Image*. 1991. Harmondsworth, UK: Arkana, 1993 ed.

Baring-Gould, Sabine. *Curious Myths of the Middle Ages*. New York, NY: University Books, 1967.

Barnstone, Willis (ed.). *The Other Bible: Ancient Esoteric Texts*. New York, NY: Harper and Row, 1984.

Baroja, Julio Caro. *The World of Witches*. Chicago, IL: University of Chicago Press, 1965.

Barraclough, Geoffrey, and Norman Stone (eds.). *The Times Atlas of World History*. 1978. Maplewood, NJ: Hammond, 1989 ed.

Baumgartner, Anne S. *A Comprehensive Dictionary of the Gods: From Abaasy to Zvoruna*. New York, NY: University Books, 1984.

Bauvel, Robert, and Adrian Gilbert. *The Orion Mystery: Unlocking the Secrets of the Pyramids*. New York, NY: Three Rivers Press, 1995.

Bayley, Harold. *Archaic England: An Essay in Deciphering Prehistory From Megalithic Monuments, Earthworks, Customs, Coins, Placenames, and Faerie Superstitions*. London, UK: Chapman and Hall, 1920.

Beard, Henry, and Christopher Cerf. *The Official Politically Correct Dictionary and Handbook*. New York, NY: Villard Books, 1993.

Bede. *Historia Ecclesiastica Gentis Anglorum* (*A History of the English Church and People*, Leo Sherley-Price, trans.). C.E. 731. Harmondsworth, UK: Penguin, 1955 (1974 ed.).

Begg, Ean. *The Cult of the Black Virgin*. Harmondsworth, UK: Arkana, 1985.

Bell, Robert E. *Women of Classical Mythology: A Biographical Dictionary*. 1991. Oxford, UK: Oxford University Press, 1993 ed.

Besant, Annie. *Esoteric Christianity or the Lesser Mysteries*. London, UK: Theosophical Publishing Society, 1905.

Best, Robert M. *Noah's Ark and the Ziusudra Epic: Sumerian Origins of the Flood Myth*. Fort Myers, FL: Enlil Press, 1999.

Bhagavad Gita (Juan Mascaró, trans.). c. 500 BC. Harmondsworth, UK: Penguin, 1962.

Biedermann, Hans. *Dictionary of Symbolism: Cultural Icons and the Meanings Behind Them* (James Hulbert, trans.). 1989. New York, NY: Facts On File, 1992 ed.

Bierlein, John Francis. *Parallel Myths*. New York, NY: Ballantine Wellspring, 1994.

Binder, Pearl. *Magic Symbols of the World*. London, UK: Hamlyn, 1972.

Boardman, John, Jasper Griffin, and Oswyn Murray (eds.). *The Roman World*. 1986. Oxford, UK: Oxford University Press, 1988 ed.

Boates, Karen Scott (ed.). *The Goddess Within*. Philadelphia, PA: Running Press, 1990.

Boorstin, Daniel J. *The Discovers: A History of Man's Search to Know His World and Himself*. 1983. New York, NY: Vintage, 1985 ed.

Bostwick, Arthur Elmore (ed.). *Doubleday's Encyclopedia*. 1931. New York, NY: Doubleday, Doran, and Co., 1939 ed.

Bouquet, Alan Coates. *Comparative Religion: A Survey and Comparison of the Great Religions of the World*. London, UK: Penguin, 1942.

Bowden, John. *Archaeology and the Bible*. Austin, TX: American Atheist Press, 1982.

Branston, Brian. *Gods of the North*. London, UK: Thames and Hudson, 1955.

Bratton, Fred Gladstone. *Myths and Legends of the Ancient Near East: Great Stories of the Sumero-Akkadian, Egyptian, Ugaritic-Canaanite, and Hittite Cultures*. New York, NY: Thomas Y. Crowell, 1970.

Breasted, James Henry. *Ancient Records of Egypt*. 5 vols. Chicago: IL: University of Chicago Press, 1906.

Brewster, Harold Pomeroy. *Saints and Festivals of the Christian Church*. New York, NY: Frederick A. Stokes, 1904.

Bridgwater, William (ed.). *The Columbia-Viking Desk Encyclopedia*. 1953. New York, NY: Viking Press, 1968 ed.

Briffault, Robert Stephen. *The Mothers: The Matriarchal Theory of Social Origins*. 1927. New York, NY: Macmillan, 1931 (single volume, abridged) ed.

Briggs, Katherine. *The Vanishing People: Fairy Lore and Legends*. New York, NY: Pantheon, 1978.

Brownrigg, Ronald. *Who's Who in the New Testament*. 1971. New York, NY: Oxford University Press, 1993 ed.

Bucke, Richard Maurice. *Cosmic Consciousness: A Study in the Evolution of the Human Mind*. 1901. New York, NY: Dutton, 1969 ed.

Budapest, Zsuzsanna Emese. *The Holy Book of Women's Mysteries* (Part 1). 1979. Oakland, CA: Susan B. Anthony Coven No. 1, 1982 ed.

———. *The Holy Book of Women's Mysteries* (Part 2). 1980. Oakland, CA: Susan B. Anthony Coven No. 1, 1982 ed.

Budge, Ernest Alfred Wallis. *Egyptian Magic*. London, UK: Kegan, Paul, Trench, Trübner, and Co., 1901.

———. *Osiris and the Egyptian Resurrection*. Vol. 1. London, UK: Philip Lee Warner, 1911.

———. *Amulets and Talismans*. 1930. New York, NY: Citadel, 1992 ed.

Bulfinch, Thomas. *Bulfinch's Mythology: The Age of Fable, the Age of Chivalry, Legends of Charlemagne*. New York, NY: Thomas Y. Crowell, 1913.

Bullough, Vern L., and Bonnie Bullough. *The Subordinate Sex: A History of Attitudes Toward Women*. 1973. Baltimore, MD: Penguin, 1974 ed.

Burn, A. R. *The Pelican History of Greece*. 1965. Harmondsworth, UK: Penguin, 1968 ed.

Burne, Jerome (ed.). *Chronicle of the World*. Mount Kisco, NY: Ecam Publications, 1989.

Butler, Trent C. (gen. ed.). *Holman Bible Dictionary*. Nashville, TN: Holman Bible Publishers, 1991.

Caesar, Gaius Julius. *The Conquest of Gaul* [*Gallic War*] (S. A. Handford, trans.). 51 B.C.E. Harmondsworth, UK: Penguin, 1951, 1988 ed.

Calvocoressi, Peter. *Who's Who in the Bible*. 1987. Harmondsworth, UK: Penguin, 1990 ed.

Campbell, Joseph. *The Masks of God: Primitive Mythology.* Vol. 1. 1959. Harmondsworth, UK: Arkana, 1991 ed.

———. *The Masks of God: Oriental Mythology.* Vol. 2. 1962. Harmondsworth, UK: Arkana, 1991 ed.

———. *The Masks of the Gods: Occidental Mythology.* Vol. 3. 1964. Harmondsworth, UK: Arkana, 1991 ed.

———. *The Masks of the Gods: Creative Mythology.* Vol. 4. 1968. Harmondsworth, UK: Arkana, 1991 ed.

———. *Myths to Live By.* New York, NY: Bantam, 1972.

———. *The Power of Myth* (with Bill Moyers). New York, NY: Doubleday, 1988.

———. *Transformations of Myth Through Time.* New York, NY: Harper and Row, 1990.

Campanelli, Pauline. *Ancient Ways: Reclaiming Pagan Traditions.* 1991. St. Paul, MN: 1992 ed.

Camphausen, Rufus C. *The Encyclopedia of Erotic Wisdom.* Rochester, VT: Inner Traditions International, 1991.

Carlyon, Richard. *A Guide to the Gods: An Essential Guide to World Mythology.* New York, NY: Quill, 1981.

Carpenter, Edward. *Pagan and Christian Creeds: Their Origin and Meaning*: New York, NY: Blue Ribbon, 1920.

Carson, Anne. *Goddesses and Wise Women: The Literature of Feminist Spirituality, An Annotated Bibliography (1980-1992).* Freedom, CA: Crossing Press, 1992.

Carter, Jesse Benedict. *The Religious Life of Ancient Rome: A Study in the Development of Religious Consciousness, From the Foundation of the City Until the Death of Gregory the Great.* Boston, MA: Houghton Mifflin, 1911.

Cassius, Dio. *The Roman History: The Reign of Augustus* (Ian Scott-Kilvert, trans.). C. 214-226. Harmondsworth, UK: Penguin, 1988.

Cavendish, Richard. *A History of Magic.* 1987. Harmondsworth, UK: Arkana, 1990 ed.

Chetwynd, Tom. *Dictionary of Sacred Myth* ("Language of the Unconscious," Vol. 3). London, UK: Aquarian Press, 1986.

Christie-Murray, David. *A History of Heresy.* Oxford, UK: Oxford University Press, 1976.

Cirlot, J. E. *A Dictionary of Symbols.* 1962. New York, NY: Philosophical Library, 1983 ed.

Collins, Sheila D. *A Different Heaven and Earth: A Feminist Perspective on Religion.* Valley Forge, PA: Judson Press, 1974.

Comay, Joan. *Who's Who in the Old Testament (Together with the Apocrypha).* 1971. New York, NY: Oxford University Press, 1993 ed.

Condon, R. J. *Our Pagan Christmas.* Austin, TX: American Atheist Press, 1989.

Constable, George (ed.). *Mysteries of the Unknown: Mystic Places.* Richmond, VA: Time-Life Books, Inc., 1987.

Cotterell, Arthur. *A Dictionary of World Mythology.* 1979. New York, NY: Oxford University Press, 1990 ed.

———. *The Macmillan Illustrated Encyclopedia of Myths and Legends.* New York, NY: Macmillan, 1989.

Cross, Frank L., and Elizabeth A. Livingstone. *The Oxford Dictionary of the Christian Church.* 1957. London, UK: Oxford University Press, 1974 ed.

Crossley-Holland, Kevin. *The Norse Myths.* New York, NY: Pantheon, 1980.

Cumont, Franz Valéry Marie. *The Mysteries of Mithra.* New York, NY: Dover, 1956.

———. *Oriental Religions in Roman Paganism.* New York, NY: Dover, 1956.

———. *Astrology and Religion Among the Greeks and Romans.* New York,

NY: Dover, 1960.

Curtis, Vesta Sarkhosh. *Persian Myths: The Legendary Past*. Austin, TX: University of Texas Press, 1993.

Dalley, Stephanie (trans.). *Myths From Mesopotamia: Creation, the Flood, Gilgamesh, and Others*. 1989. Oxford, UK: Oxford University Press, 2008 ed.

Daly, Mary. *Beyond God the Father: Toward a Philosophy of Women's Liberation*. Boston, MA: Beacon Press, 1973.

Darlison, Bill. *The Gospel and the Zodiac: The Secret Truth About Jesus*. New York, NY: Overlook Press, 2008.

Davidson, Gustav. *A Dictionary of Angels*. 1967. New York, NY: The Free Press, 1971 ed.

Davidson, Hilda Roderick Ellis. *Gods and Myths of Northern Europe*. 1964. London, UK: Penguin, 1990 ed.

Davis, Frederick Hadland. *Myths and Legends of Japan*. 1913. Mineola, NY: Dover, 1992 ed.

———. *Pagan Scandinavia*. New York, NY: Frederick A. Praeger, 1967.

———. *Gods and Myths of the Viking Age*. New York, NY: Bell, 1981.

———. *Myths and Symbols in Pagan Europe: Early Scandinavian and Celtic Religions*. Syracuse, NY: Syracuse University Press, 1988.

Davis, John J. *Biblical Numerology: A Basic Study of the Use of Numbers in the Bible*. 1968. Grand Rapids, MI: Baker Book House, 1988 ed.

Day, Michael H. *Fossil Man*. 1970. New York, NY: Bantam, 1971 ed.

Decker, Ed, and Dave Hunt. *The God Makers: A Shocking Expose of What the Mormon Church Really Believes*. Eugene, OR: Harvest House, 1984.

Delaney, John J. *Pocket Dictionary of Saints*. 1980. New York, NY: Image, 1983 (abridged) ed.

Delehaye, Hippolyte. *The Legends of the Saints: An Introduction to Hagiography.* New York, NY: Fordham University Press, 1962.

Dennis, Rabbi Geoffrey W. *The Encyclopedia of Jewish Myth, Magic and Mysticism.* Woodbury, MN: Llewellyn, 2007.

Derk, Francis H. *A Pocket Guide to the Names of Christ.* 1969. Minneapolis, MN: Bethany House, 1976 ed.

De Rosa, Peter. *Vicars of Christ.* New York, NY: Crown Publishers, 1988.

de Volney, Constantin François. *The Ruins, or, A Survey of the Revolutions of Empires.* 1791. London, UK: James Watson, 1857 ed.

de Voragine, Jacobus. *The Golden Legend, or Lives of the Saints.* 7 vols. C. 1260. London, UK: J. M. Dent and Co., 1900.

Didron, M. *Christian Iconography; or, The History of Christian Art in the Middle Ages.* 2 vols. London, UK: Henry G. Bohn, 1851.

Dione, R. L. *Is God Supernatural?: The 4,000-Year Misunderstanding.* New York, NY: Bantam, 1976.

Doane, Thomas William. *Bible Myths and Their Parallels in Other Religions.* New York, NY: University Books, 1971.

Dorward, David. *Scottish Surnames: A Guide to the Family Names of Scotland.* Glasgow, Scotland: Harper Collins, 1995.

Dowley, Tim (ed.). *The History of Christianity.* 1977. Oxford, UK: Lion Publishing, 1990 ed.

Downing, Christine. *The Goddess: Mythological Images of the Feminine.* New York, NY: Crossroads Publishing, 1984.

Durant, Will. *The Story of Civilization: Volume 1—Our Oriental Heritage.* 1935. New York, NY: Simon and Schuster, 1954 ed.

Eban, Abba. *Heritage: Civilization and the Jews.* New York, NY: Summit, 1984.

Egyptian Book of the Dead, The (E. A. Wallis Budge, trans.). 1895. New York, NY: Dover, 1967 ed.

Ehrlich, Eugene. *Amo, Amas, Amat, and More.* New York, NY: Perennial Library, 1985.

Eisler, Riane. *The Chalice and the Blade: Our History, Our Future.* New York, NY: Perennial, 1987.

Elder, Dorothy. *From Metaphysical to Mystical: A Study of the Way.* Denver, CO: Doriel Publishing Co., 1992.

Eliade, Mircea. *Images and Symbols: Studies in Religious Symbolism.* 1952. Princeton, NJ: Princeton University Press, 1991 ed.

———. *The Sacred and the Profane: The Nature of Religion* (Willard R. Trask, trans.). 1957. San Diego, CA: Harvest/Harcourt, Brace, and Jovanovich, 1959 ed.

———. *A History of Religious Ideas: From Gautama Buddha to the Triumph of Christianity* (Willard R. Trask, trans.). Vol. 2. 1978. Chicago, IL: The University of Chicago Press, 1982 ed.

Eliot, Alexander. *The Universal Myths: Heroes, Gods, Tricksters, and Others.* New York, NY: Meridian, 1976.

Ellis, Peter Berresford. *A Dictionary of Irish Mythology.* 1987. Oxford, UK: Oxford University Press, 1992 ed.

Elliot, Neil. *Sensuality in Scandinavia.* New York, NY: Weybright and Talley, 1970.

Elton, Charles Isaac. *Origins of English History.* London, UK: Bernard Quaritch, 1890.

Encyclopedia Britannica: A New Survey of Universal Knowledge. 1768. Chicago, IL/London, UK: Encyclopedia Britannica, 1955 ed.

Eusebius (of Caesarea). *The History of the Church* (G. A. Williamson, trans; Andrew Louth, ed.). Circa C.E. 315-325. Harmondsworth, UK: Penguin, 1965 (1989 ed.).

Evans, Bergen. *Dictionary of Mythology.* 1970. New York, NY:

Laurel, 1991 ed.

Evans, Elizabeth Edson. *The Christ Myth: A Study*. New York, NY: Truth Seeker Co., 1900.

Farmer, David Hugh. *The Oxford Dictionary of Saints*. 1978. Oxford, UK: Oxford University Press, 1992 ed.

Farrell, Deborah, and Carole Presser (eds.). *The Herder Symbol Dictionary: Symbols from Art, Archaeology, Mythology, Literature, and Religion* (Boris Matthews, trans.). 1978. Wilmette, IL: Chiron, 1990 ed.

Ferguson, George. *Signs and Symbols in Christian Art*. 1954. London, UK: Oxford University Press, 1975 ed.

Feuerstein, Georg. *Sacred Sexuality: Living the Vision of the Erotic Spirit*. 1992. New York, NY: Tarcher, 1993 ed.

Fideler, David. *Jesus Christ, Sun of God: Ancient Cosmology and Early Christian Symbolism*. Wheaton, IL: Quest, 1993.

Fillmore, Charles, and Theodosia DeWitt Schobert. *Metaphysical Bible Dictionary*. Unity Village, MO: Unity School of Christianity, 1931.

Finegan, Jack. *Light from the Ancient Past: The Archaeological Background of the Hebrew-Christian Religion* (Vol. 1). 1946. Princeton, NJ: Princeton University Press, 1974 ed.

Finger, Ben, Jr. *Concise World History*. New York, NY: Philosophical Library, 1959.

Fischer, Carl. *The Myth and Legend of Greece*. Dayton, OH: George A. Pflaum, 1968.

Ford, Guy Stanton (ed.-in-chief). *Compton's Pictured Encyclopedia*. 1922. Chicago: F. E. Compton and Co., 1957 ed.

Forrest, M. Isidora. *Offering to Isis: Knowing the Goddess Through Her Sacred Symbols*. St. Paul, MN: Llewellyn, 2005.

Fox, Matthew. *The Coming of the Cosmic Christ : The Healing of Mother Earth and the Birth of a Global Renaissance*. New York, NY:

Harper and Row, 1988.

Fox, Robin Lane. *Pagans and Christians*. New York, NY: Knopf, 1986.

———. *The Unauthorized Version: Truth and Fiction in the Bible*. New York, NY: Knopf, 1991.

Frazer, Sir James George. *The Golden Bough: A Study in Magic and Religion*. 1922. New York, NY: Collier, 1963 (abridged) ed.

———. *Folklore in the Old Testament*. New York, NY: Tudor Publishing, (abridged) 1923.

Freke, Timothy, and Peter Grandy. *The Jesus Mysteries: Was the Original Jesus a Pagan God?* New York, NY: Three Rivers Press, 1999.

———. *Jesus and the Lost Goddess: The Secret Teachings of the Original Christians*. New York, NY: Three Rivers Press, 2002.

Freud, Sigmund. *Totem and Taboo*. 1918. New York, NY: Vintage, 1946 ed.

———. *The Future of an Illusion*. 1928. New York, NY: W. W. Norton, 1961 ed.

———. *Civilization and Its Discontents* (James Strachey, trans.). 1930. New York, NY: W. W. Norton, 1962 ed.

———. *New Introductory Lectures Psychoanalysis*. Lecture no. 35: "A Philosophy of Life," 1932.

Gantz, Jeffrey (trans.). *Early Irish Myths and Sagas*. 1981. Harmondsworth, UK: Penguin, 1988 ed.

Gaskell, G. A. *Dictionary of All Scriptures and Myths*. 1960. New York, NY: Julian Press, 1973 ed.

Gelling, Peter, and Hilda Ellis Davidson. *The Chariot of the Sun and Other Rites and Symbols of the Northern Bronze Age*. New York, NY: Frederick A. Praeger, 1969.

Gimbutas, Marija Alseikait. *The Goddesses and Gods of Old Europe:*

Myths and Cult Images. 1974. Berkeley, CA: University of California Press, 1992 ed.

———. *The Civilization of the Goddess: The World of Old Europe* (Joan Marler, ed.). New York, NY: HarperCollins, 1991.

Glyn, Anthony. *The British: Portrait of a People*. New York, NY: G. P. Putnam's Sons, 1970.

Goldenberg, Naomi. *The Changing of the Gods: Feminism and the End of Traditional Religions*. Boston, MA: Beacon Press, 1979.

Gordon, Richard Stuart. *The Encyclopedia of Myths and Legends*. 1993. London, UK: Headline, 1994 ed.

Goring, Rosemary (ed.). *Larousse Dictionary of Beliefs and Religions*. 1992. Edinburgh, Scotland: Larousse, 1995 ed.

Graham, Lloyd M. *Deceptions and Myths of the Bible*. 1975. New York, NY: Citadel Press, 1990 ed.

Grant, Michael, and John Hazel. *Who's Who in Classical Mythology*. 1973. New York, NY: Oxford University Press, 1993 ed.

Graves, Kersey. *The World's Sixteen Crucified Saviors, or, Christianity Before Christianity: Containing New, Startling, and Extraordinary Revelations in Religious History, which Disclose the Oriental Origin of All the Doctrines, Principles, Precepts, and Miracles of the Christian New Testament, and Furnishing a Key for Unlocking Many of Its Sacred Mysteries, Besides Comprising the History of Sixteen Heathen Crucified Gods*. Boston, MA: Colby and Rich, 1876.

Graves, Robert. *The White Goddess: A Historical Grammar of Poetic Myth*. 1948. New York, NY: Noonday Press, 1991 ed.

———. *The Greek Myths*. 1955. Harmondsworth, UK: Penguin, 1992 combined ed.

Graves, Robert, and Raphael Patai. *Hebrew Myths: The Book of Genesis*. 1964. New York, NY: Anchor, 1989 ed.

Gray, John. *Near Eastern Mythology: Mesopotamia, Syria, and Palestine*.

London, UK: Hamlyn, 1963.

Green, John Richard. *A Short History of the English People* (Vol. 1). London, UK: Macmillan and Co., 1892.

Greenberg, Gary. *The Bible Myth: The African Origins of the Jewish People*. Secaucus, NJ: Citadel Press, 1996.

———. *101 Myths of the Bible: How Ancient Scribes Invented Biblical History*. Naperville, IL: Sourcebooks, 2000.

Grimal, Pierre. *The Penguin Dictionary of Classical Mythology* (A. R. Maxwell-Hyslop, trans.). 1951. Harmondsworth, UK: Penguin, 1990 ed.

Grotjahn, Martin. *The Voice of the Symbol*. Los Angeles, CA: Mara Books, 1971.

Gruss, Edmond C. *What Every Mormon Should Know*. 1975. Denver, CO: Accent, 1976 ed.

Guignebert, Charles. *The Christ* (Peter Ouzts and Phyllis Cooperman, trans.). 1943. New York, NY: Citadel, 1968 ed.

Guthrie, William K. C. *The Greeks and Their Gods*. Boston, MA: Beacon Press, 1955.

Hadas, Moses (ed.). *A History of Rome*. Garden City, NY: Doubleday Anchor, 1956.

Haining, Peter. *Witchcraft and Black Magic*. New York, NY: Grosset and Dunlap, 1972.

Hall, Eleanor L. *The Moon and the Virgin: Reflections on the Archetypal Feminine*. New York, NY: Harper and Row, 1980.

Hall, John Richard Clark. *A Concise Anglo-Saxon Dictionary*. 1894. Toronto, Canada: University of Toronto Press (and the Medieval Academy of America), 1960 ed. (1996 imprint).

Hall, Manly P. *The Secret Teachings of All Ages*. 1925. Los Angeles, CA: The Philosophical Research Society, 1989 ed.

Halliday, William Reginald. *Greek and Roman Folklore*. New York,

NY: Cooper Square, 1963.

Hamilton, Edith. *The Greek Way*. 1930. New York, NY: Mentor, 1959 ed.

———. *The Roman Way*. 1932. New York, NY: Mentor, 1961 ed.

———. *Mythology: Timeless Tales of Gods and Heroes*. 1940. New York, NY: Mentor, 1963 ed.

Hardon, John A. *Pocket Catholic Dictionary*. 1980. New York, NY: Image, 1985 ed.

Harrison, Michael. *The Roots of Witchcraft*. Secaucus, NJ: Citadel Press, 1974.

Haskins, Susan. *Mary Magdalene: Myth and Metaphor*. New York, NY: Harcourt Brace and Co., 1993.

Heidel, Alexander. *The Gilgamesh Epic and Old Testament Parallels*. Chicago, IL: University of Chicago Press, 1949.

Heindel, Max. *Nature Spirits and Nature Forces*. Oceanside, CA: Rosicrucian Fellowship, 1937.

Herm, Gerhard. *The Celts: The People Who Came Out of the Darkness*. New York, NY: St. Martin's Press, 1976.

Hinnells, John R. (ed.). *Persian Mythology*. London, UK: Hamlyn, 1973.

———. *The Penguin Dictionary of Religions: From Abraham to Zoroaster*. 1984. Harmondsworth, UK: Penguin, 1986 ed.

Hodson, Geoffrey. *The Hidden Wisdom in the Holy Bible*. Vol. 1. 1967. Wheaton, IL: Quest/Theosophical Publishing House, 1978 ed.

———. *The Hidden Wisdom in the Holy Bible*. Vol. 2. 1967. Wheaton, IL: Quest/Theosophical Publishing House, 1978 ed.

Hoeller, Stephan A. *Jung and the Lost Gospels: Insights into the Dead Sea Scrolls and the Nag Hammadi Library*. 1989. Wheaton, IL: Quest, 1990 ed.

Holroyd, Stuart. *The Arkana Dictionary of New Perspectives*.

Harmondsworth, UK: Arkana, 1989.

Hooke, S. K. *Middle Eastern Mythology: From the Assyrians to the Hebrews*. 1963. Harmondsworth, UK: Penguin, 1991 ed.

Hopfe, Lewis M. *Religions of the World*. 1976. New York, NY: Macmillan, 1987 ed.

Hoyland, Robert G. *Arabia and the Arabs: From the Bronze Age to the Coming of Islam*. London, UK: Routledge, 2001.

Hutchinson, Richard Wyatt. *Prehistoric Crete*. 1962. Harmondsworth, UK: Penguin, 1968 ed.

Hutton, Ronald. *The Pagan Religions of the Ancient British Isles: Their Nature and Legacy*. 1991. Oxford, UK: Blackwell, 2000 ed.

Huxley, Francis. *The Way of the Sacred*. New York, NY: Doubleday, 1974.

Ide, Arthur Frederick. *Yahweh's Wife: Sex in the Evolution of Monotheism*. Las Colinas, TX: Monument Press, 1991.

Jabbar, Mailk H. *The Astrological Foundation of the Christ Myth*. 4 vols. Dayton, OH: Rare Books Distributor, 1995-2003.

Jackson, John G. *Christianity Before Christ*. Austin, TX: American Atheist Press, 1985.

James, Peter, and Nick Thorpe. *Ancient Inventions*. New York, NY: Ballantine, 1994.

Johns, June. *Black Magic Today*. London, UK: New English Library, 1971.

Johnson, Robert A. *She: Understanding Feminine Psychology*. 1976. New York, NY: Perennial, 1977 ed.

Johnson, Walter, and William Wright. *Neolithic Man in North-East Surrey*. London, UK: Elliot Stock, 1903.

Jonas, Hans. *The Gnostic Religion: The Message of the Alien God and the Beginnings of Christianity*. 1958. Boston, MA: Beacon Press, 2001 ed.

Jones, Gwyn. *A History of the Vikings*. 1968. Oxford, UK: Oxford

University Press, 1984 ed.

Jones, Prudence, and Nigel Pennick. *A History of Pagan Europe*. London, UK: Routledge, 1995.

Josephus: Complete Works (William Whiston, trans.). Circa 1st to 2nd Centuries C.E. Grand Rapids, MI: Kregel Publications, 1960, 1980 ed.

Julian of Norwich. *Revelations of Divine Love*. 1373. Harmondsworth, UK: Penguin, 1966 ed.

Jung, Carl Gustav. *Man and his Symbols*. 1964. New York, NY: Dell, 1968 ed.

Keller, Werner. *The Bible As History: A Confirmation of the Book of Books* (William Neil, trans.). 1956. New York, NY: Bantam, 1980 ed.

Kelly, Sean, and Rosemary Rogers. *Saints Preserve Us!: Everything You Need to Know About Every Saint You'll Ever Need*. New York, NY: Randon House, 1993.

Kelsey, Morton T., and Barbara Kelsey. *Sacrament of Sexuality: The Spirituality and Psychology of Sex*. Warwick, NY: Amity House, 1986.

Kinsley, David. *The Goddesses' Mirror: Visions of the Divine From East and West*. Albany, NY: State University of New York Press, 1989.

Kirk, G. S. *The Nature of the Greek Myths*. 1974. Harmondsworth, UK: Penguin, 1978 ed.

Klein, Peter (ed.). *The Catholic Source Book*. Dubuque, IA: Brown-Roa, 2000.

Knight, Richard Payne. *A Discourse On the Worship of Priapus, and Its Connection With the Mystic Theology of the Ancients*. London, UK: privately printed, 1865 ed.

——. *The Symbolic Language of Ancient Art and Mythology*. New York, NY: J. W. Bouton, 1892.

Koran, The (George Sale, trans.). 1734. London, UK: Frederick Warne and Co. Ltd., n.d.

Knight, Sirona. *Exploring Celtic Druidism: Ancient Magick and Rituals for Personal Empowerment.* Franklin Lakes, NJ: Career Press, 2001.

Kramer, Heinrich, and Jakob Sprenger. *Malleus Maleficarum.* 1486. New York, NY: Dover, 1971.

Kramer, Samuel Noah. *History Begins at Sumer: Thirty-Nine Firsts in Recorded History.* 1956. Philadelphia, PA: University of Pennsylvania Press, 1981 ed.

Kuhn, Alvin Boyd. *A Rebirth For Christianity.* 1970. Wheaton, IL: Quest, 2005.

Lacy, Norris J. (ed.). *The Arthurian Encyclopedia.* New York, NY: Garland Publishing, 1986.

Laistner, Max Ludwig Wolfram. *Christianity and Pagan Culture in the Later Roman Empire.* Ithaca, NY: Cornell University Press, 1951.

Lamsa, George M. *The Holy Bible: From Ancient Eastern Manuscripts.* 1933. Philadelphia, PA: A. J. Holman, 1968 ed.

Larousse Encyclopedia of Mythology, New. 1959. London, UK: Hamlyn, 1976 ed.

Lass, Abraham H., David Kiremidjian, and Ruth M. Goldstein. *The Dictionary of Classical, Biblical, and Literary Allusions.* New York, NY: Fawcett Gold Medal, 1987.

LaVey, Anton Szandor. *The Satanic Bible.* New York, NY: Avon, 1969.

Layton, Bentley. *The Gnostic Scriptures: Ancient Wisdom for the New Age.* 1987. New York, NY: Anchor, 1995 ed.

Leakey, Richard E., and Roger Lewin. *Origins Reconsidered: In Search of What Makes Us Human.* New York, NY: Doubleday, 1992.

Leeming, David Adams. *The World of Myth.* 1990. Oxford, UK:

Oxford University Press, 1992 ed.

——. *Jealous Gods and Chosen People: The Mythology of the Middle East.* New York, NY: Oxford University Press, 2004.

Legge, Francis. *Forerunners and Rivals of Christianity.* 2 vols. New York, NY: University Books, 1964.

LeLoup, Jean-Yves. *The Gospel of Mary Magdalene.* Rochester, VT: Inner Traditions, 2002.

——. *The Gospel of Philip: Jesus, Mary Magdalene, and the Gnosis of Sacred Union.* Rochester, VT: Inner Traditions, 2004.

——. *The Gospel of Thomas: The Gnostic Wisdom of Jesus.* Rochester, VT: Inner Traditions, 2005.

Lerner, Gerda. *The Creation of Patriarchy.* 1986. Oxford, UK: Oxford University Press, 1987 ed.

Levi. *The Aquarian Gospel of Jesus the Christ: The Philosophic and Practical Basis of the Religion of the Aquarian Age of the World and of the Church Universal.* Marina Del Ray, CA: DeVorss and Co., 1982.

Lewis, Harvey Spencer. *Mansions of the Soul: The Cosmic Conception.* 1930. San Jose, CA: Ancient Mystical Order Rosae Crucis (AMORC), 1969 ed.

Lilly, William. *Christian Astrology.* 3 vols. 1647. New York, NY: Cosimo, 2005 ed.

Lindsay, Jack. *The Origins of Astrology.* New York, NY: Barnes and Noble, 1971.

Littleton, C. Scott (ed). *Mythology: The Illustrated Anthology of World Myth and Storytelling.* London, UK: Duncan Baird Publishers, 2002.

Lockyer, Herbert. *All the Women of the Bible.* Grand Rapids, MI: Zondervan, n.d.

Loetscher, Lefferts A. (ed.-in-chief). *Twentieth Century Encyclopedia of Religious Knowledge.* 2 vols. Grand Rapids, MI: Baker

Book House, 1955.

Lost Books of the Bible and the Forgotten Books of Eden, The. Iowa Falls, IA: World Bible Publishers, 1926.

Luckey, Thomas D. *Radiation Hormesis*. Boca Raton, FL: CRC Press, 1991.

Ludlow, Daniel H. (ed.). *Encyclopedia of Mormonism: The History, Scripture, Doctrine, and Procedure of the Church of Jesus Christ of Latter-Day Saints*. New York, NY: Macmillan, 1992.

Lurker, Manfred. *The Gods and Symbols of Ancient Egypt*. 1974. New York, NY: Thames and Hudson, 1984 ed.

———. *Dictionary of Gods and Goddesses, Devils and Demons* (G. L. Campbell, trans.). 1984. London, UK: Routledge, 1988 ed.

MacCana, Proinsias. *Celtic Mythology*. London, UK: Hamlyn, 1970.

MacLysaght, Edward. *The Surnames of Ireland*. 1985. Dublin, Ireland: Irish Academic Press, 1999 ed.

Malachi, Tau. *Gnosis of the Cosmic Christ: A Gnostic Christian Kabbalah*. St. Paul, MN: Llewellyn, 2005.

———. *Living Gnosis: A Practical Guide to Gnostic Christianity*. St. Paul, MN: Llewellyn, 2005.

———. *St. Mary Magdalene: The Gnostic Tradition of the Holy Bride*. St. Paul, MN: Llewellyn, 2006.

Mann, Nicholas R. *The Isle of Avalon: Sacred Mysteries of Arthur and Glastonbury*. London, UK: Green Magic, 2001.

Marcus, Rebecca B. *Prehistoric Cave Paintings*. New York, NY: Franklin Watts, 1968.

Markale, Jean. *Cathedral of the Black Madonna: The Druids and the Mysteries of Chartres*. Rochester, VT: Inner Traditions, 2004.

Maspero, Gaston. *Popular Stories of Ancient Egypt*. New York, NY: University Books, 1967.

Massey, Gerald. *The Historical Jesus, and the Mythical Christ: Natural*

Genesis and Typology of Equinoctial Christolatry. 1883. New York, NY: Cosimo, 2006 ed.

———. *Ancient Egypt: The Light of the World*. 12 vols. London, UK: T. Fisher Unwin, 1907.

Matthews, Caitlín and John. *The Encyclopedia of Celtic Wisdom: A Celtic Shaman's Sourcebook*. Rockport, MA: Element, 1994.

Matthews, John. *The Winter Solstice: The Sacred Traditions of Christmas*. Wheaton, IL: Quest, 2003.

McArthur, Tom (ed.). *The Oxford Companion to the English Language*. Oxford, UK: Oxford University Press, 1992.

McConkie, Bruce R. *Mormon Doctrine*. 1966. Salt Lake City, UT: Bookcraft, 1992 ed.

McKenzie, John L. *Dictionary of the Bible*. New York, NY: Collier, 1965.

McKinsey, C. Dennis. *The Encyclopedia of Biblical Errancy*. Amherst, NY: Prometheus, 1995.

McLean, Adam (ed.). *A Treatise on Angel Magic: Magnum Opus Hermetic Sourceworks*. 1989. York Beach, ME: Weiser, 2006 ed.

Mead, George Robert Stow. *Thrice-Greatest Hermes: Studies in Hellenistic Theosophy and Gnosis*. London, UK: Theosophical Publishing Society, 1906.

———. *The Mysteries of Mithra*. London, UK: Theosophical Publishing Society, 1907.

Mead, Frank Spencer, and Samuel S. Hill. *Handbook of Denominations in the United States*. 1951. Nashville, TN: Abingdon Press, 1989 ed.

Mead, Margaret. *Male and Female: A Study of the Sexes in a Changing World*. 1955. New York, NY: Mentor, 1959 ed.

Meredith, Joel. *Meredith's Book of Bible Lists*. Minneapolis, MN: Bethany House, 1980.

Metford, J. C. J. *Dictionary of Christian Lore and Legend.* London, UK: Thames and Hudson, 1983.

Metzger, Bruce M., and Michael D. Coogan (eds.). *The Oxford Companion to the Bible.* New York, NY: Oxford University Press, 1993.

Meurois-Givaudan, Anne and Daniel. *The Way of the Essenes: Christ's Hidden Life Remembered.* Rochester, VT: Destiny, 1992.

Miller, Malcolm. *Chartres Cathedral.* New York, NY: Riverside Book Co., 1997.

Mills, A. D. *Oxford Dictionary of English Place-names.* 1991. Oxford, UK: Oxford University Press, 1998 ed.

Mish, Frederick (ed.). *Webster's Ninth New Collegiate Dictionary.* Springfield, MA: Merriam-Webster, 1984 ed.

Mollenkott, Virginia Ramey. *The Divine Feminine: The Biblical Imagery of God as Female.* New York, NY: Crossroad Publishing, 1993.

Monaghan, Patricia. *The Book of Goddesses and Heroines.* 1990. St. Paul, MN: Llewellyn, 1991 ed.

Monroe, Douglas. *The 21 Lessons of Merlyn: A Study in Druid Magic and Lore.* St. Paul, MN: Llewellyn, 1992.

Montagu, Ashley. *The Natural Superiority of Women.* 1952. New York, NY: Collier, 1992 ed.

Morehead, Albert H. (ed.). *The Illustrated World Encyclopedia.* 1954. Woodbury, NY: Bobley Publishing, 1977 ed.

Morgan, Elaine. *The Descent of Woman.* 1972. New York, NY: Bantam, 1973 ed.

Nelson, Thomas (pub.). *Nelson's New Compact Illustrated Bible Dictionary.* 1964. Nashville, TN: Thomas Nelson, 1978 ed.

Neumann, Erich. *The Great Mother: An Analysis of the Archetype* (Ralph Manheim, trans.). New York, NY: Pantheon, 1955.

Newall, Venetia. *The Encyclopedia of Witchcraft and Magic.* New

York, NY: A and W Visual Library, 1974.
Norton-Taylor, Duncan. *The Emergence of Man: The Celts.* New York, NY: Time-Life, 1974.
O'Brien, Arthur. *Europe Before Modern Times: An Ancient and Medieval History.* 1940. Chicago, IL: Loyola University Press, 1943 ed.
Odent, Michael. *Water and Sexuality.* Harmondsworth, UK: Arkana, 1990.
O'Flaherty, Wendy Doniger. *Hindu Myths.* Harmondsworth, UK: Penguin, 1975.
Olson, Carl (ed.). *The Book of the Goddess, Past and Present: An Introduction to Her Religion.* New York, NY: Crossroad, 1983.
Orme, A. R. *Ireland* (from "The World's Landscapes" series, James M. Houston, ed). Chicago, IL: Aldine, 1970.
Osborne, John. *Britain.* New York, NY: Time-Life, 1963.
Oxford English Dictionary, The (compact edition, 2 vols.). 1928. Oxford, UK: Oxford University Press, 1979 ed.
Pagels, Elaine. *The Gnostic Gospels.* 1979. New York, NY: Vintage, 1981 ed.
———. *Adam, Eve, and the Serpent.* 1988. New York, NY: Vintage, 1989 ed.
———. *The Origin of Satan.* New York, NY: Random House, 1995.
Patai, Raphael. *The Hebrew Goddess.* 1967. Detroit, MI: Wayne State University Press, 1990 ed.
Paulsen, Kathryn. *The Complete Book of Magic and Witchcraft.* 1970. New York, NY: Signet, 1980 ed.
Pearson, Carol S. *Awakening the Heroes Within: Twelve Archetypes to Help Us Find Ourselves and Transform Our World.* New York, NY: HarperCollins, 1991.
Pennick, Nigel. *The Pagan Book of Days: A Guide to the Festivals,*

Traditions, and Sacred Days of the Year. Rochester, VT: Destiny, 1992.

Pepper, Elizabeth, and John Wilcock. *Magical and Mystical Sites: Europe and the British Isles.* Grand Rapids, MI: Phanes Press, 1992.

Perowne, Stewart. *Roman Mythology.* 1969. Twickenham, UK: Newnes Books, 1986 ed.

Pinch, Geraldine. *Egyptian Mythology: A Guide to the Gods, Goddesses, and Traditions of Ancient Egypt.* Oxford, UK: Oxford University Press, 2004.

Prahbupada, A. C. Bhaktivedanta Swami. *Beyond Birth and Death.* Los Angeles, CA: The Bhaktivedanta Book Trust, 1979.

Prophet, Elizabeth Clare. *Mary Magdalene and the Divine Feminine: Jesus' Lost Teachings on Woman - How Orthodoxy Suppressed Jesus' Revolution for Woman and Invented Original Sin.* Gardiner, MT: Summit University Press, 2005.

Qualls-Corbett, Nancy. *The Sacred Prostitute: Eternal Aspect of the Feminine.* Toronto, Canada: Inner City Books, 1988.

Rabb, Theodore K. *The Struggle for Stability in Early Modern Europe.* New York, NY: Oxford University Press, 1975.

Raftery, Barry. *Pagan Celtic Ireland: The Enigma of the Irish Iron Age.* London, UK: Thames and Hudson, 1994.

Ramm, Bernard L. *Hermeneutics.* 1967. Grand Rapids, MI: Baker Book House, 1988 ed.

Reaney, P. H., and R. M. Wilson. *A Dictionary of English Surnames.* 1958. Oxford, UK: Oxford University Press, 1997 ed.

Reed, Ellen Cannon. *Circle of Isis: Ancient Egyptian Magic for Modern Witches.* Franklin Lakes, NJ: Career Press, 2002.

Regula, deTraci. *The Mysteries of Isis: Her Worship and Magick.* 1995. St. Paul, MN: Llewellyn, 2001 ed.

Reilly, Patricia Lynn. *A God Who Looks Like Me: Discovering a Woman-*

        Affirming Spirituality. New York, NY: Ballantine, 1995.

Roberts, R. Philip. *Mormonism Unmasked: Confronting the Contradictions Between Mormon Beliefs and True Christianity*. Nashville, TN: Broadman and Holman, 1998.

Robertson, John M. *Christianity and Mythology*. London, UK: Watts and Co., 1900.

———. *A Short History of Christianity*. London, UK: Watts and Co., 1902.

———. *Pagan Christs: Studies in Comparative Hierology*. London, UK: Watts and Co., 1903.

———. *Pagan Christs*. 1966. New York, NY: Dorset Press, 1987 ed.

Robinson, James M (ed.). *The Nag Hammadi Library in English*. 1978. San Francisco, CA: Harper Collins, 1990 ed.

Rocco, Sha. *Sex Mythology*. 1898. Austin, TX: American Atheist Press, 1982 ed.

Rufus, Anneli S., and Kristan Lawson. *Goddess Sites: Europe*. New York, NY: HarperCollins, 1991.

Runciman, Steven. *A History of the Crusades: Vol. 1, The First Crusade and the Foundation of the Kingdom of Jerusalem*. 1951. New York, NY: Harper Torchbooks, 1964 ed.

Runes, Dagobert D. (ed.). *Dictionary of Judaism*. 1959. New York, NY: Citadel Press, 1991 ed.

Russell, Bertrand. *Why I Am Not a Christian: and Other Essays on Religion and Related Subjects*. New York, NY: Touchstone, 1957.

Rutherford, Ward. *Celtic Mythology: The Nature and Influence of Celtic Myth—From Druidism to Arthurian Legend*. New York, NY: Sterling, 1990.

Salmonson, Jessica Amanda. *The Encyclopedia of Amazons: Women Warriors from Antiquity to the Modern Era*. New York, NY: Paragon House, 1991.

Schwartz, Howard. *Gabriel's Palace: Jewish Mystical Tales.* New York, NY: Oxford University Press, 1993.

——. *Tree of Souls: The Mythology of Judaism.* Oxford, UK: Oxford University Press, 2004.

Scott, George Ryley. *Phallic Worship: A History of Sex and Sexual Rites.* London, UK: Senate, 1996.

Seabrook, Lochlainn. *The Goddess Dictionary of Words and Phrases: Introducing a New Core Vocabulary for the Women's Spirituality Movement.* 1997. Nashville, TN: Sea Raven Press, 2010 ed.

——. *The Book of Kelle: An Introduction to Goddess-Worship and the Great Celtic Mother-Goddess Kelle, Original Blessed Lady of Ireland.* 1999. Franklin, TN: Sea Raven Press, 2010 ed.

——. *Christmas Before Christianity: How the Birthday of the "Sun" Became the Birthday of the "Son."* Franklin, TN: Sea Raven Press, 2010.

——. *Everything You Were Taught About the Civil War is Wrong, Ask a Southerner!* 2010. Franklin, TN: Sea Raven Press, revised 2014 ed.

——. *Jesus and the Law of Attraction: The Bible-Based Guide to Creating Perfect Health, Wealth, and Happiness Following Christ's Simple Formula.* Spring Hill, TN: Sea Raven Press, 2013.

——. *The Bible and the Law of Attraction: 99 Teachings of Jesus, the Apostles, and the Prophets.* Spring Hill, TN: Sea Raven Press, 2013.

——. *Jesus and the Gospel of Q: Christ's Pre-Christian Teachings As Recorded in the New Testament.* Spring Hill, TN: Sea Raven Press, 2014.

——. *Autobiography of a Non-Yogi: A Scientist's Journey From Hinduism to Christianity* (Dr. Amitava Dasgupta, with Lochlainn Seabrook). Spring Hill, TN: Sea Raven Press, 2015.

——. *Seabrook's Bible Dictionary of Traditional and Mystical Christian*

Doctrines. Spring Hill, TN: Sea Raven Press, 2016.

———. *Confederate Flag Facts: What Every American Should Know About Dixie's Southern Cross*. Spring Hill, TN: Sea Raven Press, 2016.

———. *The Goddess Encyclopedia of Secret Words, Names, and Places*. Unpublished manuscript.

———. *Seabrook's Complete Encyclopedia of Deities*. Unpublished manuscript.

———. *The Unauthorized Encyclopedia of the Bible*. Unpublished manuscript.

———. *The Complete Dictionary of Christian Mythology*. Unpublished manuscript.

Seznec, Jean. *The Survival of the Pagan Gods*. Princeton, NJ: Princeton University Press, 1953.

Shah, Amina. *Arabian Fairy Tales*. London, UK: Octagon Press, 1989.

———. *Tales From the Bazaars of Arabia: Folk Stories From the Middle East*. London, UK: Octagon Press, 2002.

Shaw, Ian (ed.). *The Oxford History of Ancient Egypt*. 2000. Oxford, UK: Oxford University Press, 2002 ed.

Sherfey, Mary Jane. *The Nature and Evolution of Female Sexuality*. 1972. New York, NY: Vintage, 1973 ed.

Simons, Gerald. *Barbarian Europe* (from the *Great Ages of Man* series). New York, NY: Time-Life, 1968.

Sjöö, Monica, and Barbara Mor. *The Great Cosmic Mother: Rediscovering the Religion of the Earth*. New York, NY: Harper and Row, 1987.

Skelton, Robin, and Margaret Blackwood. *Earth, Air, Fire, Water: Pre-Christian and Pagan Elements in British Songs, Rhymes and Ballads*. Harmondsworth, UK: Arkana, 1990.

Smith, Lacey Baldwin. *This Realm of England: 1399 to 1688*. 1966.

Lexington, MA: D. C. Heath and Co., 1983 ed.

Smith, William. *Smith's Bible Dictionary.* Circa 1880s. Nashville, TN: Thomas Nelson, 1986 ed.

Sobol, Donald J. *The Amazons of Greek Mythology.* Cranbury, NJ: A.S. Barnes and Co., 1972.

Spence, Lewis. *Ancient Egyptian Myths and Legends.* 1915. New York, NY: Dover, 1990 ed.

——. *An Encyclopedia of Occultism.* 1920. New York, NY: Citadel Press, 1993 ed.

——. *The History and Origins of Druidism.* 1949. New York, NY: Samuel Weiser, 1971 ed.

Starbird, Margaret. *The Goddess in the Gospels: Reclaiming the Sacred Feminine.* Rochester, VT: Bear and Co., 1998.

——. *Magdalene's Lost Legacy: Symbolic Numbers and the Sacred Union in Christianity.* Rochester, VT: Bear and Co., 2003.

Stark, Rodney. *Discovering God: The Origins of the Great Religions and the Evolution of Belief.* New York, NY: HarperCollins, 2007.

Stein, Diane. *The Goddess Book of Days.* 1988. Freedom, CA: The Crossing Press, 1992 ed.

Stetkevych, Jaroslav. *Muhammad and the Golden Bough: Reconstructing Arabian Myth.* Bloomington, IN: Indiana University Press, 1996.

Stone, Merlin. *When God was a Woman.* San Diego, CA: Harvest, 1976.

——. *Ancient Mirrors of Womanhood: A Treasury of Goddess and Heroine Lore from Around the World.* 1979. Boston, MA: Beacon Press, 1990 ed.

Strachan, Gordon. *Chartres: Sacred Geometry, Sacred Space.* Edinburgh, Scotland: Floris Books, 2003.

Streep, Peg. *Sanctuaries of the Goddess: The Sacred Landscapes and Objects.* Boston, MA: Bullfinch Press, 1994.

Strong, James. *Strong's Exhaustive Concordance of the Bible.* 1890. Nashville, TN: Abingdon Press, 1975 ed.

Sturluson, Snorri. *The Prose Edda.* Berkeley, CA: University of California Press, 1954.

Swindoll, Cynthia (ed.). *Abraham: Friend of God.* 1986. Fullerton, CA: Insight for Living, 1988 ed.

Sykes, Egerton. *Who's Who in Non-Classical Mythology.* 1952. New York, NY: Oxford University Press, 1993 ed.

Szekely, Edmond Bordeaux. *The Essene Gospel of Peace.* 1937. Nelson, B.C., Canada: International Biogenic Society, 1981 ed.

Telushkin, Rabbi Joseph. *Jewish Literacy.* New York, NY: William Morrow and Co., 1991.

Tenney, Merrill C. (gen. ed.). *Handy Dictionary of the Bible.* Grand Rapids, MI: Lamplighter, 1965.

The Epic of Gilgamesh (N. K. Sandars, ed.). Circa 3000 BCE. Harmondsworth, UK: Penguin, 1960 (1972 ed.).

The Fossil Record and Evolution. Collected articles from *Scientific American.* San Francisco, CA: W. H. Freeman and Co., 1982 ed.

The Golden Treasury of Myths and Legends (adapted by Anne Terry White). New York, NY: Golden Press, 1959.

Thompson Chain-Reference Bible, The. King James Version. Indianapolis: B. B. Kirkbride Bible Co., 1964.

Thompson, James Westfall, and Edgar Nathaniel Johnson. *An Introduction to Medieval Europe: 300-1500.* New York, NY: W. W. Norton, 1937.

Thorsten, Geraldine. *God Herself: The Feminine Roots of Astrology.* New York, NY: Avon, 1981.

Tompkins, Peter. *Secrets of the Great Pyramid.* 1971. New York, NY: Harper Colophon, 1978 ed.

Towns, Elmer L. *The Names of Jesus*. Denver, CO: Accent, 1987.

Trevelyan, George Macaulay. *History of England: Vol. 1, From the Earliest Times to the Reformation*. 1926. Garden City, NY: Anchor, 1952 ed.

Traupman, John C. *The New College Latin and English Dictionary*. 1966. New York, NY: Bantam, 1988 ed.

——. *The Bantam New College German and English Dictionary*. 1981. New York, NY: Bantam, 1986 ed.

Tripp, Edward. *History of England: Vol. 2, The Tudors and the Stuart Era*. 1926. Garden City, NY: Anchor, 1952 ed.

——. *The Meridian Handbook of Classical Mythology*. 1970. Harmondsworth, UK: Meridian, 1974 ed.

Turcan, Robert. *The Cults of the Roman Empire*. 1992. Oxford, UK: Blackwell, 2000 ed.

Udry, J. Richard. *The Social Context of Marriage*. 1966. Philadelphia, PA: J. B. Lippincott, 1974 ed.

Van De Mieroop, Marc. *A History of the Ancient Near East, ca. 3000-323 BC*. 2004. Oxford, UK: Blackwell, 2007 ed.

Vermaseren, Maarten J. *Cybele and Attis*. London, UK: Thames and Hudson, 1977.

Vermes, Geza (ed.). *The Dead Sea Scrolls in English*. 1962. Harmondsworth, UK: Penguin, 1987 ed.

von Daniken, Erich. *Chariots of the Gods?: Unsolved Mysteries of the Past*. 1968. New York, NY: Bantam, 1973 ed.

——. *Gods from Outer Space: Return to the Stars*, or *Evidence for the Impossible*. 1968. New York, NY: Bantam, 1974 ed.

Walker, Barbara G. *The Woman's Encyclopedia of Myths and Secrets*. San Francisco, CA: Harper and Row, 1983.

——. *The Crone: Woman of Age, Wisdom, and Power*. San Francisco, CA: Harper and Row, 1985.

——. *The Woman's Dictionary of Symbols and Sacred Objects*. San

Francisco, CA: Harper and Row, 1988.

Walum, Laurel Richardson. *The Dynamics of Sex and Gender: A Sociological Perspective*. Chicago, IL: Rand McNally College Publishing, 1977.

Watts, Alan. *Behold the Spirit: A Study in the Necessity of Mystical Religion*. 1947. New York, NY: Random House, 1971 ed.

Way, George, and Romilly Squire. *Scottish Clan and Family Encyclopedia*. Glasgow, Scotland: HarperCollins, 1994.

Webster's Ninth New Collegiate Dictionary. Springfield, MA: Merriam-Webster, 1984 ed.

Weigall, Arthur. *The Life and Times of Akhnaton: Pharaoh of Egypt*. London, UK: W. Blackwood and Sons, 1910.

———. *Wanderings in Anglo-Saxon Britain*. New York, NY: George H. Doran, 1926.

———. *The Paganism in Our Christianity*. New York, NY: G. P. Putnam's Sons, 1928.

White, Jon Manchip. *Ancient Egypt: Its Culture and History*. 1952. New York, NY: Dover, 1970 ed.

———. *Everyday Life in Ancient Egypt*. 1963. New York, NY: Perigree, 1980 ed.

White, R. J. *The Horizon Concise History of England*. New York, NY: American Heritage, 1971.

Wilde, Lady. *Irish Cures, Mystic Charms, and Superstitions* (compiled by Sheila Anne Barry). New York, NY: Sterling Publishing, 1991.

Wilkinson, Richard H. *The Complete Temples of Ancient Egypt*. London, UK: Thames and Hudson, 2000.

———. *The Complete Gods and Goddesses of Ancient Egypt*. London, UK: Thames and Hudson, 2003.

Wind, Edgar. *Pagan Mysteries in the Renaissance*. New York, NY: W. W. Norton, 1968.

Winick, Charles. *Dictionary of Anthropology*. Totowa, NJ: Littlefield, Adams and Co., 1970.

Winks, Robin W., Crane Brinton, John B. Christopher, and Robert Lee Wolff. *A History of Civilization, Vol. 1: Prehistory to 1715*. 1955. Englewood Cliffs, NJ: Prentice Hall, 1988 ed.

Witt, Reginald Eldred. *Isis in the Ancient World*. 1971. Baltimore, MD: John Hopkins University Press, 1997.

Woolger, Jennifer Barker, and Roger J. Woolger. *The Goddess Within: A Guide to the Eternal Myths that Shape Women's Lives*. 1987. New York, NY: Fawcett Columbine, 1989.

Wright, John W. (ed.). *The Universal Almanac, 1994*. Kansas City, MO: Andrews and McMeel, 1993.

Young, Dudley. *Origins of the Sacred: The Ecstasies of Love and War*. 1991. New York, NY: Harper Perennial, 1992 ed.

Young, G. Douglas (gen. ed.). *Young's Compact Bible Dictionary*. 1984. Wheaton, IL: Tyndale House, 1989 ed.

Zaehner, R. C. (ed.) *Encyclopedia of the World's Religions*. 1959. New York, NY: Barnes and Noble, 1997 ed.

Zimmerman, J. E. *Dictionary of Classical Mythology*. New York, NY: Bantam, 1964.

Zondervan (publisher). *Zondervan Compact Bible Dictionary*. 1967. Grand Rapids, MI: Zondervan, 1993 ed.

 INDEX

abdomens	29
Abnoba (Goddess)	108
Achall (Goddess)	73, 108
Achill Head, Ireland	73
Achill Island, Ireland	73
Achill, Ireland	73
Achtan (Goddess)	108
Acionna (Goddess)	108
Actland (Goddess)	108
adoration	43
Adsullata (Goddess)	108
adversary	94
Aegeans, the	75
Aeracura (Goddess)	108
Aerfen (Goddess)	54, 108
Aeron (Goddess)	108
Aerten	108
Aerten (Goddess)	108
Aertha (Goddess)	70
Aetna (Goddess)	66
Aetna, Mount (Italy)	66
Aeval (Goddess)	108
Afra (Goddess)	70
Africa	2, 14, 31, 70, 115, 128
Agape, the	102
Agrona (Goddess)	108
Aibheaog (Goddess)	72, 108
Aid-Woman	87
Aife (Goddess)	59, 108
Aige (Goddess)	74
Ailinn (Goddess)	108
Aimend (Goddess)	108
Ain (Goddess)	108
Aine (Goddess)	109
Airmed (Goddess)	109

Al-Lat (Goddess) 91, 93-95
Al-Uzza (Goddess) 91
Alaisiagae (Goddess) 109
alba 60
Alba (Goddess) 68
Alba (Scotland) 60
Alba, Italy 39, 68
Alban, Saint 39
Albania 39, 61, 68
Albania (Scotland) 61
Albania (the Balkans) 39, 68
Albannaich 61
albe 60
Albi, France 39, 68
Albia, Princess 38
Albina (Goddess) 38
Albion (England) 37
Albion (Goddess) 37-39, 60, 62, 68, 83
Albiones 37, 38
Albion's Land 61
albus 37
Aldborough, England 43
All Hallows 63
All Saints Day 63
all-female Holy Trinity 93
Allah (God) 91, 95
Almha (Goddess) 74, 109
Almu (Goddess) 74
Alphito (Goddess) 38
Amashilamma (Goddess) 86
Amazonia 59
Amazonian Queen 59
Amazonian Queen-Goddess, Scottish 59
Amor (Goddess) 89
Amorites, the 89, 90
Ana (Goddess) 42
Ana-Badb-Macha (Goddess) 42

Anat (Goddess) 96
Anath (Goddess) 96
Anatolia, Goddess-worship in 96
Ancamma (Goddess) 109
Ancasta (Goddess) 109
ancient Egypt 93, 134, 135, 138, 141, 145
Andarta (Goddess) 109
Andraste (Goddess) 43, 109
androcentricity 21
Andromeda (Goddess) 69
Andros (God) 60
angel 135
angels 11, 51, 53, 122
Angles, the 51, 53, 76
Angleslant 53
Angli, the 51, 53
Anglo-Celtic culture 105
Anglo-Celtic Goddess myths 103
Anglo-Celtic Goddess statuary 102
Anglo-Celtic goddesses 103
Anglo-Celtic mythology 89
Anglo-Celtic place-names 102
Anglo-Celtic society 22
Anglo-Saxon invasions 46
Angurboda (Goddess) 75
animals 64
Anna (Goddess) 76
Anne (Goddess) 109
Annea Clivana (Goddess) 109
Anu (Goddess) 74, 109
Aoibhell (Goddess) 109
Aoife (Goddess) 59
Aphro (Goddess) 70
Aphrodite (Goddess) 52
apple 92
apple blossom, sacred to Goddess 92
apple, as sacred fruit of Goddess 92

Aquae Sulis 48
Aquinas, Thomas 17
Arabia, Goddess-worship in 96
Arabia, matriarchal 91
Arabia, Patriarchal Takeover in 95
Arabian Mother-Goddess 95
Arabian mythology 91
archaeologists 28, 107
archaeology 28, 118, 125
archetypal females 29
archetypes 137
Ardwina (Goddess) 109
Argante (Goddess) 109
Argive people 38
Ariadne (Goddess) 109
Arianrhod (Goddess) 109
Arnamentia (Goddess) 109
Art (God) 69
Artemis (Goddess) 69
Arthur, King 49, 69
Artio (Goddess) 69, 109
Asherah (Goddess) 86, 90, 95-97
Ashesh (Goddess) 95
Ashnan (Goddess) 95
Ashtoreth (Goddess) 90
Asia (continent) 8, 69
Asia (Goddess) 70
Astarte (Goddess) 86, 94, 96
astrology 121, 133, 143
astronomical calendar 35
Athaliah, Queen, Hebrew Goddess-worshiper 96
Athena (Goddess) 67
Athene (Goddess) 67
Athens, Greece 67
Athtar (Goddess) 96
Attart (Goddess) 96
Au Set (Goddess) 95

Audhumbla (Goddess)	86
Aufaniae (Goddess)	109
Aughty (Goddess)	73
Aurora (Goddess)	66
Aurora Borealis	66
Austria	97
Autobiography of a Non-Yogi (Dasgupta and Seabrook)	140
Aveta (Goddess)	109
Baal (God)	93
Baaltis (Goddess)	93
Babylonia	89, 96
Babylonia, Goddess-worship in	96
Babylonian Goddess-worship	75
Babylonians	96
Badb (Goddess)	42, 109
Balkans, the	39
Ban Naomha (Goddess)	109
Ban-Chuideachaidh Moire (Goddess)	87, 109
Banba (Goddess)	71, 109
Bandonga (Goddess)	109
Bandua (Goddess)	109
Banshee (Goddess)	103, 109
Bantry Bay, Ireland	73
baptism	102
Basilea (Goddess)	77, 109
basilica	77, 93
Bath, England	48
bats	64
battle	2, 43
Bay of Aige, Ireland	74
Ba'Alat (Goddess)	93
Bé Chuille (Goddess)	109
Beag (Goddess)	109
Bean Nighe (Goddess)	109
bear (Goddess symbolism)	69
Bear-God	69
Bear-Goddess	69

Beare Island, Ireland 73
Bebhionn (Goddess) 109
Becuma (Goddess) 109
Bede 37
beginnings and endings 33
Belili (Goddess) 93
Belisama (Goddess) 54
Belisima (Goddess) 109
Bellona (Goddess) 66
Benvarry (Goddess) 109
Berecyntia (Goddess) 109
Bergusia (Goddess) 109
Bernard of Clairvaux 17
Berne, Switzerland 68, 69
Bible . . . 3, 18, 90, 116, 118, 119, 122, 123, 125-129, 131-136, 140-143,
146, 197, 201
Biddy (Goddess) 87, 109
Biddy Early (Goddess) 73
Biddy Mannion (Goddess) 109
Bird-Goddess, Irish 74
birds 3
birth 15, 33, 42, 70, 75, 77, 79, 125, 132, 138
birth and death 33
birth-life-death cycle 42
Bithidh a'bhandia leat 103
Black Agnes (Goddess) 76
Black Annis (Goddess) 61, 76, 109
Black Annis' Bower 76
Black Lake 73
Black-Queen-Goddess 61
Blathnat (Goddess) 49, 109
blessing 102
Blodeuwedd (Goddess) 49
Blodewedd (Goddess) 109
blood 2, 116
Bloody [lunar] Crescent 47
Blue Hag, the (Goddess) 76

Bo Dhu (Goddess) 85
Bo Find (Goddess) 85, 86, 109
Bo Ruadh (Goddess) 85
Boand (Goddess) 72
Boann (Goddess) 72, 85, 109
boiling 42
Bone Mother 61
Bormana (Goddess) 109
Bothar-bó-finné 85
Boudicca, Queen, of the Iceni Tribe 43
Bouvinda (Goddess) 85
box 6
Boyne River (Ireland) 72
Branwen (Goddess) 52, 109
breast symbolism 32, 75
breast, female 33
breast-milk, Goddess' 83
breasts 29, 74, 75
Breasts of Anu 74
Brent River (England) 43, 54
Bretagne 46
Breton language 46
Bretons, the 46
Bri (Goddess) 109
Briant (Goddess) 54
Briant River (England) 54
Bricta (Goddess) 109
Bride (Goddess) 45, 110
bride (marital) 45
Bride River (Ireland) 72
Bride, Saint 87
Bridewell (England) 102
Bridget, Saint 87, 89
Bridgit (Goddess) 41
brig 46
brigade 46
brigadier 46

brigand 46
Brigandu (Goddess) 46
Brigantes, the 43
Brigantia (Goddess) 33, 43, 45, 46, 87-89, 97, 98, 102, 110
Brigantia, Empire of 41
Brigantia's Well 102
brigantine 46
Bright Arrow 41
Bright One 41
Brigid (Goddess) 41-46, 59, 72, 97, 110
Brigid's religion 44
Bringer of Light 94, 95
Britain 11, 19, 22, 23, 28, 31, 38, 45, 51, 53, 57, 66, 93, 137, 145
Britannia (Goddess) 45, 97, 105, 110
Britannus Secunda 57
British Isles 21, 27, 28, 31, 41, 42, 46, 76, 87, 103, 107, 108
British Isles, Goddess-worship in 92
British legends 38
British myth 61
British tribes 43
British "experts" 22
British-Celtic mythology 49
Brito 46
Briton 46
Britons 11, 32-34, 39, 43, 83, 89, 105
Britons, ancient 34, 39
Britons, Christian 89
Britons, modern 105
Brittany 46, 92
Broad Face 69
Bronach (Goddess) 72, 110
Bronwen (Goddess) 52
Bronze Age 76, 126, 130
Bronze Age tribes 76
broom 62
Buan (Goddess) 110
Buddhism 89

Burren, the, Ireland 72
buttocks 29
Cabrillo, Juan 62
Caer (Goddess) 73, 110
Cailainn (Goddess) 72
Caileach Cinn Boirne (Goddess) 72
Cailleach (Goddess) 72, 110
Cailleach Bheur (Goddess) 61
Cailleach na Mointeach 35
Caillech (Goddess) 61, 62
Caireen (Goddess) 110
Caledonia 61
Caledonii, the 62
Califia (Goddess) 62
California, USA 62
Callanish Standing Stones 58
Callanish, Scotland 34
Cally (Goddess) 62
Cally Berry (Goddess) 61, 110
Camma (Goddess) 110
Campestres (Goddess) 110
Canaan 115
Candlemas 102
canoes 66
Canola (Goddess) 74, 110
canola, grain 74
Caolainn (Goddess) 110
Cappadocia 66
Car (Goddess) 92
Cara (Goddess) 91
Carlin (Goddess) 61-64, 110
Carman (Goddess) 110
Carna (Goddess) 91, 92
Carnival, Goddess festival 93
Carravogue (Goddess) 110
Carrawburgh River (England) 54
Carrig Cliodna, Ireland 74

Carthage, Africa 60
Cartimandua (Goddess) 110
Cartimandua, Queen 43
Cassiopeia (Goddess) 69
Castalia (Goddess) 69
Castalides (Goddess) 69
Cat Ana (Goddess) 76
Catherine of Siena 17
Catholic Church 15
Catholicism 76
Catholics 16, 98
Cathubodia (Goddess) 71, 110
cats 3, 64
cats, black 64
Cattle-Goddess, Irish 86
cave 76, 81, 134
cave paintings 134
cave symbolism 81
cave-shrine 76
Ceann Cailighe (Goddess) 72
Ceasg (Goddess) 62, 110
Ceibhfhionn (Goddess) 110
Celestial Father 48
cell 81
Celtai 81
Celtic Britain 66
Celtic Britons 33, 43, 83
Celtic Cross, the 102
Celtic customs 41
Celtic Goddess-worship 77
Celtic myth 69
Celtic tribes 37, 69
Celtic tribes, in ancient Turkey 82
Celtic-Britons, and Goddess-worship 43
Celto-Teutonic Goddess 59
Celts 9, 21, 41, 44, 47, 59, 81, 82, 85, 105, 129, 137
Celts in England 42

Celts, modern 105
Ceres (Goddess) 91
Cerridwen (Goddess) 38, 58, 110
Cessair (Goddess) 110
Cethlion (Goddess) 110
Cetnenn (Goddess) 110
chalice 124
chariot 126
Chartres Cathedral 136
cheese 86
children 2, 15, 17, 62, 64
children's fairy tales 62
Chlaus Haistic (Goddess) 110
Chloë (Goddess) 77
Christ (God) 78
Christian Church 16, 53, 63, 76-78, 118, 121
Christian Church, adopts Pagan Samhain 63
Christian Church, and practice of "converting" Pagan deities 53
Christian Church, anti-female legends in Ireland 76
Christian denominations 15
Christian Fathers 87
Christian mystics 17
Christian mythographers 88
Christian mythology 48, 49, 141
Christian nations 21
Christian symbolism 78, 125
Christian tradition 17, 115
Christian underworld 67
Christianity . . . 3, 14, 15, 17-19, 44, 48, 60, 66, 87, 93-95, 98, 115, 117,
             123-125, 127, 130, 132-134, 139, 140, 142, 145, 201
Christianity, in Ireland 77
Christianity, patriarchal 44, 93
Christianity, star-goddess of 94
Christianization process 39, 46, 60, 78, 81, 102
Christians 18, 19, 39, 75, 91, 97, 126
Christians, Gnostic 75
Christmas 3, 15, 63, 102, 115, 121, 135, 140, 201

Christmas (originally a Goddess Holy Day) 102
Christmas Before Christianity (Seabrook) 140
Christmas Before Christianity (Seabrook) 15
church architecture, English 102
circle 102, 138
circles 12, 32
circular monuments 32
Civil War 2, 3, 59, 140, 197
classical authorities 28
Claudius, Emperor 45
Cleonae, the 65
Cleone (Goddess) 65
Clidna (Goddess) 74, 110
Clidna's Waves 74
Cliodna (Goddess) 74
Clota (Goddess) 110
Clutoida (Goddess) 54
Clyde River (England) 54
Cocidius (Goddess) 110
comparative religion 118
compatriots 57
Condwiramur (Goddess) 110
Confederate Flag 59
Confederate Flag Facts (Seabrook) 59
consort, male (of Goddess) 77
constellations, Goddess 69
Corchen (Goddess) 110
Cordelia 58
Core (Goddess) 91
Cork, Ireland 74
Cornwall 107
Corra (Goddess) 110
Cosmic Christ 125, 134
Cosmos 70
couples, and the Hieros Gamos 35
Coventia (Goddess) 110
Coventina (Goddess) 54

cow 85
Cow-Goddesses 59
Cow-Goddesses, of Ireland 85
Cow's Lake, Ireland 85
Creatress, the (Goddess) 42
Creatrix 70, 86
Creatrixes 86
Cred (Goddess) 75, 110
Creiddylad (Goddess) 58, 110
Creide (Goddess) 75
crescent Moon 33, 94
Creta (Goddess) 66
Crete (Goddess) 66
Crete (island) 66
criminal 6, 10
Criti 197
Cro-Magnon people 28
Crobdh Dearg (Goddess) 110
Crom Cruaich 47
Cromarty, Scotland 61
Crone 42, 61, 62, 65, 75, 91, 144
Crone-Goddess 61, 75, 79, 91
Crone-Goddess, Greek 65
Crone-Goddess, Scottish 61
crop circles 32
cross 2, 9, 17-19, 31, 39, 42, 59, 60, 65, 78, 83, 102, 103, 121, 141
Cross of Odin 60
Cross of Saint Andrew 60
Cross of Wotan 60
Cross, Latin 42
crown 94, 123
Crusades 139
cube 93
Cuchulain 48
curds 86
customs, Goddess 101
Cybele (Goddess) 93

Cyhiraeth (Goddess) 110
Cymidei Cymeinfoll (Goddess) 110
Cymru 57
Da (Goddess) 67, 110
Dactyls, the (Goddesses) 65
Dahut (Goddess) 110
Dainty Tease 49
Dam-Kina (Goddess) 75
Damara (Goddess) 110
Dames Vertes (Goddess) 110
Damona (Goddess) 110
Dana (Goddess) 68, 74-77, 79
Danae, ... 75
Danai, the 38
Danaids, the 38
Danaus, King 38
Dana's Fairies 76
dance, Goddess 32
Danes, the 75
Dane's Hill (England) 76
Danites, the 76
Danu (Goddess) 74, 110
Danu-Ana (Goddess) 76
Danube River 75
Danuna (Goddess) 75
Daoine Sidhe 76
Dark Goddess 62
dark hole 81
Dark Mother, the (Goddess) 53
Dark Pool 73
Dark Water 73
Darkness 91
daughter 69, 91, 94, 96
Day of Venus 52
Dea Artio (Goddess) 69
Dea Nutrix (Goddess) 110
Deae Matres (Goddess) 110

death 3, 33, 42, 49, 79, 96, 102, 120, 138
Death-Goddess 49, 102
December 67
Dechtere (Goddess) 48, 110
Dee River (England) 54
deer 67, 74
Deino (Goddess) 65
Deirdre (Goddess) 110
deities 16, 18, 41, 47, 85, 86, 95, 103, 107, 141
Delilah (Goddess) 49
Demeter (Goddess) 77
demons 64, 134
Denmark 67, 75
Dennitsa (Goddess) 75
Depth psychology 32
destiny 136, 138
Destroyer, the (Goddess) 42
Devon River (England) 54
Devona (Goddess) 54
Devorgilla (Goddess) 111
Dia Griene (Goddess) 111
Diana Lucifera (Goddess) 94
Diana Triformis (Goddess) 42
Diancecht (God) 47
Dies Veneris 52
Digi No Duineach (Goddess) 61
Dil (Goddess) 86, 111
Dinah (Goddess) 76
Diodorus 27
Disciplina (Goddess) 67
divination 64
Divine Feminine 16, 17, 19, 23, 115, 136, 138
Divine Masculine 16
divine oneness 35
Divona (Goddess) 111
Dnieper River 75
Dniestr River 75

Domnu (Goddess) 111
Don (Goddess) 74, 111
Don River 75
Donegal, County, Ireland 72
Dover, England 37
Dragon's Mouth, lake of the, Ireland 73
Drake, Sir Francis 62
Druantia (Goddess) 111
Druidry, modern 103
Druids 33, 42, 71, 103, 134
Druids, ancient 33, 42
Druids, modern 103
Dubh Lacha (Goddess) 73, 111
Dublin, Ireland 73
Dunnu (Goddess) 75
dyaus 48
Dyaus Pitar (God) 48, 90
Eadon (Goddess) 111
eagle 197
early Roman invaders 61
Earth 47, 64, 66, 67, 70, 71, 75, 77, 98, 121, 125, 141
Earth-Goddess, Celtic 47
Earth-Goddess, Irish 71
Earth-Goddess 47, 66, 71, 75
Earth-Mother 67
east 21, 118, 130, 131, 133, 141, 144
Easter 63, 102
Ebhlinne (Goddess) 73, 111
Ecclesia 15, 117
Echtghe (Goddess) 73, 111
Eckhart, Meister 17
Edain (Goddess) 111
Edinburgh, Scotland (Goddess-worship in) 45
egg 32, 117
Egypt 86, 89, 93, 118, 134, 135, 138, 141, 145
Egypt, ancient 85, 89
Egypt, ancient, Goddess-worship in 93

Egyptian mythology 138
Egyptians 95
Egyptians, ancient, Goddess-worship among 95
Éire 72
Elat (Goddess) 66
Elat, Indonesia 66
Elath (Goddess) 66
Elátia, Greece 66
Elbe River (Germany) 39, 68
elder 27, 124
Ele (Goddess) 111
Emer (Goddess) 111
England . 9, 13, 21, 23, 27, 28, 31-33, 37, 38, 41, 42, 48, 51-53, 57, 60,
 62, 71-73, 86-88, 98, 101, 103, 107, 117, 141, 144, 145
England, ancient 38
England, Queen of 101
England's national flower 103
Engles, the 53
Engles' Land 53
entrances and exits 33
Enyo (Goddess) 65
Eos (Goddess) 66
Eostre (Goddess) 111
Epiphany 93
Epona (Goddess) 111
equinox 34
Erce (Goddess) 111
Erda (Goddess) 70
Erecura (Goddess) 111
Eri of the Golden Hair (Goddess) 111
Erin (Ireland) 72
Erinn (Ireland) 72
Eriu (Goddess) 71, 111
Ernmas (Goddess) 111
Ess Euchen (Goddess) 111
Estiu (Goddess) 111
Etain (Goddess) 73, 111

eternal flame, Brigid's	44
Ethne (Goddess)	47, 111
Etruria	70
Etruscan myth	70
etymology	105
Eucharist, the	102
Europa (Goddess)	69
Europe	3, 9, 13, 14, 19, 21, 39, 47, 65, 68, 69, 71, 103, 122, 126, 127, 131, 137-139, 141, 143, 197
European Moon-Goddess	47, 68
Everything You Were Taught About the Civil War . . . (Seabrook)	59
evolution	116, 119, 130, 141-143
eye	48
Fachea (Goddess)	111
fairies	64
fairy tales	62, 141
fairy tales, children's	62
Fairy-Queen, Irish	75
Fall Equinox	63
fall harvest festival	63
Fand (Goddess)	111
fate	97
father	2, 19, 48, 58, 60, 77, 78, 90, 91, 95, 105, 122
Father (God), Christian	78
Father of Fathers	78
Father, the Son, and the Holy Spirit	78
Father-God	48, 77
Father-God, Arabian	91
Father-God, Hebrew	90
Father-God, Scandinavian	60
Father-Gods, Greek, Hebrew, and Roman	90
father-god	19, 48, 60, 90, 91, 95, 105
Fatima (Goddess)	94
Feakle Parish, Ireland	73
Feast of Epiphany	93
Feast of Ingathering	93
Feast of Our Lady of Mercy	93

Feast of the Dead	63
Feithline (Goddess)	111
female deities	41
female figures	28
Female Principle	102
female religion	22
female-based religions	27
female-based spiritual belief systems	33
feminine Deity, in Christianity	15
feminine megalithic structures, in Scotland	35
Feminine Principle	22, 32
feminine rite, ancient	35
feminine-based spiritual belief systems	22
fertility	52, 85
Fertility-Goddess	52
festivals	32, 63, 118, 137
festivals, Goddess	32
Fideal (Goddess)	111
Finchoem (Goddess)	111
Findabar (Goddess)	111
Finncaev (Goddess)	111
Fiongalla (Goddess)	111
Fionnuala (Goddess)	111
fire	9, 41, 43, 44, 72, 141
Fire-Goddess	41
Fire-Goddess, Irish	72
Fithir (Goddess)	111
five, as sacred number of Goddess	92
five-pointed star	92
Flidais (Goddess)	111
flint carvings	28
flood myth	117
Flower-face	49
folklore	126, 128
Folta (Goddess)	71
Formorians (Deities)	47
fortune	3, 33

Foster Mother of Christ	99
Fotla (Goddess)	111
fountain	38, 69
four Pagan Quarter Days	63
France	31, 39, 41, 46, 55, 68, 92, 98
Francis of Assisi	17
Frea (Goddess)	52
Freud, Sigmund	97
Freya (Goddess)	52, 60
Friatag	52
Friday (Goddess day)	52
Frigedaeg	52
Frigg (Goddess)	51
Frigga (Goddess)	51, 52
Frigga's Day	52
fruit	92
funerals, Goddess	32
Fyorgyn (Goddess)	70
Gaeldom	82
Gaels, the	82
Gaidhealtachd	82
Gaillimh inion Breasail (Goddess)	111
Gala (Goddess)	66, 82, 83
Gala, Queen	82
Gala-Tea (Goddess)	82
Galacia	107
Galahad, Sir	82
Galata, Queen (Goddess)	82
Galatea (Goddess)	66, 82
Galatia	82
Galatians, the Book of	82
galaxy	83
Gallia (Goddess)	111
games, Goddess	32
garland	132
gatekeeping God	78
Gauls, the	82

Genesis 18, 90, 115, 127, 135
Gentle Annie (Goddess) 76, 111
German Goddess-worship 76
Germanic tribes 51, 52, 76
Germans 9, 51
Germany 39
Gillagriene (Goddess) 111
Gimbutas, Marija A. 28
glamor (witch's spell) 57
Glamorgan (Wales) 57
Glas (Goddess) 85, 111
gnosis 22
Gnostic 15, 75, 78, 130, 132-134, 137
Gnostic Christianity 15
Gnostic Gospels 137
Gnostics, the (first Christians) 15, 75
God . 2, 3, 18, 19, 21, 47, 48, 58, 60, 67, 69, 77, 78, 90, 91, 93-97, 103,
  105, 115, 120, 122, 123, 125, 126, 130, 136, 138, 142,
  143
Goddess . . 3, 5-9, 13-16, 18, 19, 21, 22, 25, 27, 28, 31-35, 37-39, 41-49,
  51-54, 57-62, 65-79, 81-83, 85-98, 101-103, 105, 107,
  108, 115, 116, 118, 123, 125-127, 137, 139-142, 146,
  198, 201
Goddess of the Sacred Grove 49
Goddess religion 28, 34, 54
Goddess World 22
Goddess, eponymous 105
Goddess-oriented items 28
Goddess-worship, Aegean 75
Goddess-worship, Albanian 39
Goddess-worship, Balkan 39
Goddess-worship, Biblical 82
Goddess-worship, Breton 46
Goddess-worship, British 28, 83, 87
Goddess-worship, Danish 75
Goddess-worship, English 27, 32, 37, 39, 76, 88
Goddess-worship, European 68

Goddess-worship, Gaelic 82
Goddess-worship, German 39, 51, 76
Goddess-worship, Greek 38, 65, 75
Goddess-worship, Hebrew 76
Goddess-worship, Hindu 53
Goddess-worship, Iberian 31
Goddess-worship, Irish 71-78
Goddess-worship, Italian 39
Goddess-worship, Paleolithic 28, 29
Goddess-worship, Roman 38, 48, 52
Goddess-worship, Russian 75
Goddess-worship, Saxon 76
Goddess-worship, Scandinavian 52
Goddess-worship, Scottish 34, 35, 45, 46, 52, 58, 62, 82
Goddess-worship, Sicilian 68
Goddess-worship, Welsh 38, 52, 57
Goddess-worshiping Britons 32
Goddess-worshiping religion 46
goddesses ... 9, 13, 27, 45, 54, 57, 65, 69-72, 77, 85, 86, 91, 92, 94, 95,
            103, 105, 107, 108, 115, 120, 126, 134, 136, 138, 145
Goddesses of the British Isles 108
goddesses, English 54
Goddess' power 32
Goddess-worship ... 3, 5, 6, 9, 13, 14, 19, 21, 22, 25, 27, 32, 33, 37, 48,
            51, 53, 57, 68, 73, 77, 78, 87, 93, 96, 97, 101, 103, 105,
            107, 140, 198, 201
Godiva, Lady (Goddess) 103, 111
gods 27
Goewin (Goddess) 111
gold 2, 3, 5, 62, 132, 197
Góntia (Goddess) 111
good luck 34
grace 42
Graeae (Goddess) 65
Graeci, the 65
Graeco-Roman world 78
grain 74

Grainne (Goddess) 111
Grainne ni Malley (Goddess) 111
grandfather 27, 45
grandmother 42, 43
Grandmother, the (Goddess) 42
Gray Ones, the 65
Great Britain 19
Great Goddess 8
Great Mother 15, 28, 33, 94, 136
Great Mother-Goddess 15, 28, 33, 94
Great Queen of Phantoms 42
Great Whore of Babylon, the 97
Great Year, the Celtic 33, 44
Greece 71, 89
Greece, ancient 38, 65, 69, 86
Greek Earth-Mother Goddess 67
Greek Goddess 59
Greek mythology 142
Greeks 52, 65, 75, 81, 121, 128
Greeks, ancient 65, 75
Green Day (Goddess Holy Day) 77
Gregorian Calendar 51
Grey Eyebrows 61
Grian (Goddess) 111
Guinevere, Lady (Goddess) 103, 112
Gwyar (Goddess) 112
Gwyllion (Goddess) 112
Gypsies, the 53
Habetrot (Goddess) 112
Habondia (Goddess) 112
Hag of Black Head 72
Hag of the Iron Wood (Goddess) 75
Hag of Winter 61
Hag's Head 72
Halloween 62-64, 102
Halloween, Goddess origins of 62
Hallowmass 63

Hathor (Goddess) 86
healing, Goddess 41
health 3, 35, 54, 140, 201
Heart 91
Heaven 17, 97, 121
Heavenly Father (God) 48, 90
Hebrew Father-God 90
Hebrew Goddess-worship 76
Hebrew Mother-Goddess 95
Hebrew myths 127
Hebrew priests, as patriarchal murderers 96
Hebrew priests, patriarchal 90
Hebrew queens, who worshiped Goddess 96
Hebrew scholars 90
Hebrew women, early, and the worship of Goddess 96
Hebrews 76, 130
Hebrides (Scotland) 59
Hel (Goddess) 67
Hell 2, 67, 109
Helvetii, the 69
henge monuments 32
henges, ancient British 34
henges, stone 31
henges, wood 31
Henry VIII 44
Henwen (Goddess) 112
Hera (Goddess) 71, 86
hero 2, 48, 58
Hertha (Goddess) 70
Hieros Gamos 35
Hill of Almha, Ireland 74
Himilco 60
Hindus, the 81
historians 22
historical Jesus 134
hole 67
Holland 67

Holle (Goddess) 67
Holmhurst Hill, England 38, 39
holy days, Goddess 102
holy shrine, Goddess' 48
Holy Trinity, all-female 79
Holy Virgin 92
hominids 28
Homo erectus 28
Homo sapiens, archaic 28
hope 19
horse 73
Horse-Goddess, Celtic 73
horseshoe 33
horseshoe symbolism 33
horseshoes, hanging 34, 101
Horus (God) 95
Hrede (Goddess) 51
human societies 34
Hurria, Goddess-worship in 96
Hybla (Goddess) 68
Hybla Galeatis, Sicily 68
Hybla Heraea, Sicily 68
Hybla Major, Sicily 68
Hybla Minor, Sicily 68
Hyblaean Mountains, Sicily 68
Iahu (Goddess) 90
Iahu Anat (Goddess) 90
Ianuaria (Goddess) 112
Iberian religious shrines 31
Iberians, the 31
Icovellauna (Goddess) 112
Ilse of Lewis, Scotland 34
Inciona (Goddess) 112
India 61, 89
Inghean Bhuidhe (Goddess) 112
insemination (of the Triple-Goddess) 77
inspiration 54, 69, 88

Invincible One 43
Io (Goddess) 59
Iona (Scotland) 59
Ionians, the 59
Iouga (Goddess) 112
Iraq 89
Ireland . . . 3, 9, 13, 16, 21, 41, 44, 47, 71, 72, 74, 76, 77, 79, 82, 86, 89, 107, 134, 137, 138, 140
Ireland, Goddess-oriented 71
Ireland, original Holy Trinity in 79
Irenaeus 17
Irish 38, 42, 47-49, 61, 71-76, 81, 85, 124, 126, 134, 138, 145
Irish artisans 42
Irish Goddess-worship 76
Irish Harp 74
Irish literature, Goddess in 61
Irish myth 48, 61
Irish mythology 49
Irish Sea-Deities 47
Irish War-Goddess 42
Iron Age 21, 138
Iron Age societies 21
Ishtar (Goddess) 94, 96
Isis (Goddess) 95
Isis-Ra-El (Trinity) 95
Islam, the rise of, in matriarchal Arabia 95
Islam's religious symbol, Goddess influences on 94
Isle of Man 107
Israel 86, 89, 92, 95
Israel, ancient 86, 89
Israel, etymology of word 95
Israel, Goddess-worship at Mount Carmel 92
Isurium Brigantum 43
Isurium, etymology of 43
Italians 52
Italy 39, 66, 68, 89
Iu-Pater (God) 90

Jahi (God) 90
January 6, 93
January 1 6
January 6 93
Japan 122
Jason (God) 48
Jehovah (God) 48, 90
Jerusalem 139
Jesus (God) 97, 99
Jesus and the Gospel of Q (Seabrook) 140
Jesus and the Law of Attraction (Seabrook) 140
Jewish Christianity 15
Jewish Temple, Pagan rites connected to 96
Jewish women, ancient, practicing Pagan rites 96
Jewish-Christians, and Goddess 97
Jewish-Christians 97
Jews 18, 19, 90, 91, 97, 123
Jews, early, as a matriarchal people 90
Jews, Goddess-worshiping ancestors of the 90
Jezebel, Hebrew Goddess-worshiper 96
John Paul II 17
John the Baptist 63
Jove (God) 48, 90
Judaism 115, 139, 140
Judeo-Christian mythology 49
Judges, Book of 76
Julian of Norwich 17
Julius Caesar 27
June 6, 34, 70, 130
June, etymology of word 70
Juno (Goddess) 70
Jupiter (God) 48, 90, 95
Jutes, the 51
Kali (Goddess) 61, 81, 92
Kali Ma (Goddess) 53
Kauli (Goddess) 91
Kaur (Goddess) 91

Ka'abe, the	93
Kel-Mari (Goddess)	89
Kele-De, the	81
Kelle (Goddess)	44, 81, 92, 105
Kelley (family surname)	81
Kelle's Island (Ireland)	81
Kelle's shrines	81
Kellie (family surname)	81
Kelly (family surname)	81
Keltoi	81
Kelts, the	81
Ker (Goddess)	91
Kerry, County (Ireland)	74
key-bearing God	78
key-holding God, Christian	78
Kher (Goddess)	91
Kilda, Saint	81
Kildare, Ireland	44, 81
king	38, 42, 44, 47, 49, 58, 96, 116, 122, 127, 143, 199
King Lear	58
King Lear (Shakespeare)	58
kings	19, 90, 96, 97
Kirn	93
knowledge	22, 75
Kore (Goddess)	91-93
Koreion, Goddess festival	93
Koreshites	91
Korrigan (Goddess)	112
Kubaba, the	93
lactation	82
Lady Eriu (Goddess)	72
Lagan River (Ireland)	72
Lammas	102
Land Given by Kali	61
land of Eriu	72
Land of [the Goddess] Albion	61
Land of [the Goddess] Gala	82

Land of [the Goddess] Skadi 68
land unplowed for a year 71
Lat (Goddess) 65, 91
Late Paleolithic peoples 29
Latiaran (Goddess) 112
Latin language 98
Latin people, the 65
Latin-Mediterranean Goddess 70
Latis (Goddess) 54, 112
Latona (Goddess) 91
laurel 125, 145
Lavercam (Goddess) 112
Le Fay (Goddess) 112
Leanan Sidhe (Goddess) 112
legends 38, 86, 118, 119, 121-123, 127, 142, 143
Leicester, England 61
Leicestershire, England 76
Lent 102
Leo 117
Leto (Goddess) 91
Liban (Goddess) 112
Libra 6, 121, 124, 125, 129, 130, 137, 139
life . . . 3, 15, 32, 42, 75, 76, 79, 81, 86, 91, 92, 101, 102, 120, 121, 126,
136, 137, 141, 145
Life-and-Death-Goddess, Celtic 102
Light of the World 135
light, Moon 59
lion 123
Litavis (Goddess) 112
Little Flower 49
living beings 86
Llyr (God) 58
Logia (Goddess) 72, 112
Lombards, the 52
London, England 39, 46, 47, 102
London, surname 47
Lord 93

Lothian, Scotland 61
Lough-na-Bo, Ireland 85
Lourdes, France 55
love 2, 3, 15, 16, 51, 67, 89, 101, 108, 131, 146
Love-Goddess, Germanic 51
Luaths Lurgann (Goddess) 112
Lucifer 95
Luckey, Thomas D. 35
Lud (God) 47
Ludgate Hill (England) 48
Lud's Gate (England) 47
Lug (God) 47, 48
Lugad, Saint 48
Lugadius, King 48
lugal 47
Lugdunum 47
Lugidus, Saint 48
Lug's temple 47
Lunar beliefs 35
Lunar Calendar 34
Lunar circle 102
Lunar Crescent, as sacred symbol of Goddess 94
Lunar deity 85
Lunar events 34
Lunar religion 31
Lunar Standstill 34
Lundinium 47
Lundon, surname 47
Lundonn 46
Luther, Martin 17
Ma (Goddess) 66, 89, 97
Ma Lata (Goddess) 66
Maacah, Queen, Hebrew Goddess-worshiper 96
Mabb (Goddess) 58, 112
Macbeth (Shakespeare) 42
MacCulloch, J. A. 27
Macha (Goddess) 41, 112

MacKelly (family surname) 81
Maerin (Goddess) 89
Maeve (Goddess) 112
magic 81, 117, 119, 121, 123, 126, 128, 130, 132, 134-138
Magog (Goddess) 112
Mah (Goddess) 66
Mah-Bellona (Goddess) 66
Maid Marian (Goddess) 66, 89, 103
Maiden 91
mainstream scientists 31
major and minor female deities 107
Major Lunar Standstill 34
Mal (Goddess) 73, 112
Mala Liath (Goddess) 61, 112
male bias 23
male chieftains 31
male figures (absent in Paleolithic record) 28
male figurines, prehistoric 29
Male Principle 102
male religion 79
Malta 65
Mama (Goddess) 89
Manat (Goddess) 91
Mar (Goddess) 66, 89, 97
Mara (Goddess) 89
Marah (Goddess) 89
Marcellinus, Ammianus 27
March 17 (Goddess Holy Day) 77
Marcia Proba (Goddess) 112
Mari (Amorite city) 89
Mari (Goddess) 89, 97, 98, 112
Maria (Goddess) 66, 89, 98
Mariam (Goddess) 97
Marian (Goddess) 98
marier 98
marine 54
Maritare, ceremony of 98

Marratu (Goddess) 89
marriage 3, 52, 98, 144
marriage, etymology of connected to Goddess 98
marriage, origins of the word 98
marriage, under Goddess 52
Martu, the 90
Mary (Goddess) 97, 98
Masculine Principle 22
masculinization process 39
Mathair-Shliabh, Ireland 74
Matres (Goddess) 112
matriarchal nature of British Isles 28
matriarchal Pagan priestesses 63
matriarchal people, early Jews as a 90
matriarchal phase 21
matriarchal phase, Celtic and British 21
matriarchal rituals 44
matriarchal societies 22
Matriarchate 22
matriarchy 53
matricentric phase 23
matricentric religion, of early England 32
matricentricity, British 22
matricentricity, religious 57
matronymicism 73
May Day 102
May Eve 102
McKelly (family surname) 81
mead 135
Mecca 93
Medb (Goddess) 112
medical establishment 35
Medieval Europe 143
meditation 102
Mediterranean region 65
meetings 32
meetings, Goddess 32

Megara Hyblaea, Sicily	68
Melusine (Goddess)	112
Menat (Goddess)	91
Meri (Goddess)	89, 97
mermaid	62
Mermaid-Goddess	62
Mersey River (England)	54
Merton, Thomas	17
Mesopotamia	47, 122, 127
metal-working, and Goddess-worship	43
Middle Ages	116, 123
Middle East	133, 141
Middlesex, England	43
Midsummer	63, 102
Milk	65, 75, 82, 83, 85, 86
Milk-Goddess	82
Milk-Goddess, Celtic	82
Milky Way	83, 85
milky white	82
Miltown Malbay, Ireland	73
mind-body-spirit complex	42, 79
Minerva (Goddess)	49
Minerva Medica (Goddess)	112
miracles	127
Modron (Goddess)	112
Mohammed	94
Moher, Cliffs of, Ireland	72
Momu (Goddess)	112
Monandaeg	39
Moncha (Goddess)	112
Monday	39
Mongfind (Goddess)	112
monotheistic worship	21
mons veneris	75
Moon	3, 9, 32, 33, 35, 37-39, 46, 47, 59-62, 68, 69, 82, 83, 86, 91, 94, 96, 115, 128
Moon symbolism	33

Moon pendants 96
Moon, as sacred symbol of Virgin Mary 94
Moon-Cow-Goddess, Celtic 86
Moon-Cow-Goddesses 86
Moon-worshipping designers 32
Moon-Goddess 3, 38, 39, 47, 60, 62, 68, 69, 82, 83
Moon's Day 39
Moon's most northern path 34
Moon's most southern path 34
Mor Muman (Goddess) 112
Morgan (Goddess) 49, 57
Morgan Le Fay (Goddess) 49, 112
Morgay (Goddess) 112
Moriath (Goddess) 112
Mormons 15
Morning Star 94, 95
Morrigan, the (Goddess) 42, 112
Moruadh (Goddess) 112
Most Holy One 93
mother . . 3, 13, 15-19, 22, 28, 33, 37, 42, 45, 48, 60, 67, 70, 71, 73, 77,
                79, 81, 82, 89, 92-97, 99, 116, 125, 136, 140, 141, 201
Mother Lat 66
Mother Mountain 74
Mother of All Deities 74
Mother of the Stars (Goddess) 85
Mother of the [Witches'] Coven 54
Mother, the (Goddess) 42
Mother-Goddess, Celtic 81
Mother-Goddess, Germanic 70
Mother-Goddess, pre-Celtic 73
Mother-Goddess, Scandinavian 60
Mother-Goddess, universal 89
mother-goddesses, and the number five 92
Mother-Moon-Goddess, Celtic 37
Mothering Sunday 102
mothers 22
Mother-Earth 71, 77

Mother-Goddess   3, 13, 15, 16, 18, 19, 28, 33, 45, 48, 60, 70, 73, 81, 89,
                                                    93-95, 140, 201
Mother's Day 102
Mount Carmel, Israel 92
Mountain of Venus 75
mountain symbolism 75
Mountain-Goddess, Irish 73
Mountain-Goddess, Roman 66
Muime Chriosda (Goddess) 99, 112
Muireartach (Goddess) 112
Munanna (Goddess) 112
Muse, the (Goddess) 69
Muse-Goddess, Scandinavian 68
music 197, 199
Mycenae (ancient Greece) 69
myrrh 16, 89
Myrrha (Goddess) 89
myth   ...   2, 48, 58, 59, 61, 69, 70, 75, 95, 105, 115-117, 120, 121, 123,
                                      125, 127-130, 132, 133, 142
mythographers 60, 78, 88
mythographers, Christian 60, 78
mythology 15, 48, 49, 89, 91, 117, 119-121, 124, 125, 127-134, 138-
                                                        144, 146
Nanna (Goddess) 112
Nantosuelta (Goddess) 112
Nar (Goddess) 112
Naria (Goddess) 113
national holiday, Ireland's 77
national symbol, Ireland's 77
nature 3, 21, 28, 76, 124, 129-131, 139, 141, 197, 201
Neanderthals 28
Near East 118, 144
Near-Eastern Goddesses 91
Nehalennia (Goddess) 113
Nemain (Goddess) 113
Nemetona (Goddess) 49, 113
Neolithic Age 31

Neopaganism	103
Nessa (Goddess)	113
New Albion (USA)	62
New Testament	3, 78, 82, 118, 127, 140, 201
New Year	102
Niamh (Goddess)	113
Nicnevin (Goddess)	61, 113
Nimue (Goddess)	113
nineteen priestesses (of Brigid)	44
nineteen standing stones	33, 34
nineteen, as sacred number	33
nineteen-year Lunar cycle	35
nineteen-year cycle	35, 44
ninth swell upon the sea	74
north	2, 3, 31, 118, 130, 197
North Africa	31
North America	3
Northern hemisphere	34
numerology	33, 122
nun	75
nursery rhymes, English	86
oak	11, 45
oak trees	45
Oak-Men, the	42
Oanuava (Goddess)	113
objective scholarship	23
obscene gargoyle	102
occult	115
October	6, 63
Odin (God)	60
Odras (Goddess)	113
offerings, leaving, for Goddess	54
Old Religion	63, 103
Old Testament	121, 126, 129
Old Woman	61
Old Woman of the Moors	35
Olwen (Goddess)	113

One Who Hides 67
Oona (Goddess) 113
Origen 17
orthodox Christian Church 76
Our Lady 93
owls 64
O'Kelly (family surname) 81
Pagan Christianity 15
Pagan Christs 139
Pagan converts 15
Pagan Europe 122, 131
Pagan prototypes of Jesus 96
Pagan religions 130
Pagan symbolism 60
Paganism 15, 18, 58, 121, 145
Pagans 19, 63, 91, 126
Paleolithic Age 28
papa 78
paper 6
Paphos (ancient Greece) 82
Paps of Anu (Ireland) 74
Pater (God) 60, 78
Pater Patrum (God) 78
patriarchal Christian priests 63
patriarchal Christianity 21
patriarchal culture 48
patriarchal societies 23
Patriarchal Takeover 95
Patriarchal Takeover, in Arabia 95
patriarchalization of religion 23
patron saint, Ireland's 77
Pemphredo (Goddess) 65
Penarddun (Goddess) 113
pentacle 92, 94
pentacle, as sacred symbol of Goddess 92, 94
People of the Goddess Dana 76
people of [the Goddess] Albion 61

Persia	122, 129
Petra (God)	78
Petros (God)	78
Phallic-God	78
Phrygia	93
Phrygia, Goddess-worship in	93
pig	58
pit	48, 90
pitar	48
place-names	37
place-names, English	102
place-names, Goddess	102
planets	86
Pliny the Elder	27
poetry, Goddess	41
politics, Goddess	101
pope, origin of word	78
portal	63
Poseidon (God)	67
prayer	102
prayers	89
pre-Christian times	28
pregnancy symbolism	33
prehistory	117, 146
Preserver, the (Goddess)	42
priestesses, Brigantia's	33
priestesses, Kelle's	81
priests	63, 88, 90, 96
prophecy	54
protectress	71
Ptolemy	27
pubic triangle	28
pudenda	67
queen	42, 43, 59, 61, 75, 77, 82, 96, 101
Queen Lat	91
Queen Lat (Goddess)	91
Queen Mab	58

Queen of Heaven, title of Goddess 90, 97
queens 101
Queens, British love of 101
Q're (Goddess) 91
radiation 35, 134
radiation hormesis 35
radiation level 35
rape seed 74
Ratis (Goddess) 113
rebirth 77, 132
red-headed tribe 62
regeneration symbolism 32
Restalrig, Scotland 46
resurrection 119
Revelation 94, 95, 97
Revelation, Book of 94
Rhed-monat 51
Rheda (Goddess) 51
Rheda's Month 51
Rhiannon (Goddess) 113
Ricagumbeda (Goddess) 113
Ritona (Goddess) 113
ritual, Goddess 32
rituals 15, 102, 115, 132
rituals, Goddess 102
River Boyne, Ireland 85
Rock, the 78
Rock-God 78
rock-god, Christian 78
Roma (Goddess) 53, 65, 89
Roman Dawn-Goddess 66
Roman Empire 18, 132, 144
Roman Goddess 70
Roman troops 51
Roman, mythology 78
Romans 9, 17, 37, 43, 45, 47-49, 51, 52, 81, 90, 121
Romans, ancient, & the Celts 81

Romans, the	37, 43, 45, 47-49, 51, 52, 90
Romany (origins of word)	53
Rome	38, 65, 66, 89, 91-93, 98, 120, 128
Rome, ancient	38, 53, 65, 98
Rome, Italy	66, 89, 93
Rome, Italy, Goddess-worship in	92
Romeo and Juliet (Shakespeare)	58
Rosary, the	102
rose, the	103
Rosmerta (Goddess)	113
Ross, Scotland	61
royal tombs	31
Russia	75
Russian Goddess-worship	75
Russian myth	75
Saba (Goddess)	113
Sabbath	102
Sabbath Day, the	102
Sabrina (Goddess)	54, 113
sacred fire	44
sacred fountain, of Goddess	38
Sacred Grove	49
sacred manifestations, of Goddess	32
sacred numerology	33
sacred site, Scotland	35
sacred sites	39, 54, 55
sacred temple site	35
sacred tree	68
sacred tree groves	96
Sacred Union	35
Saint Andrew	60, 78
Saint Andrew's Cross	59
Saint Augustine	17
Saint Bridget	99
Saint Hildegard	17
Saint John of the Cross	17
Saint Kilda's Isle (Ireland)	81

Saint Patrick 77, 78, 87
Saint Patrick's Day 77
Saint Paul 8, 17, 18, 21, 78, 82, 91
Saint Peter 78
Saint Peter's Basilica 93
Saint Polycarp 17
Saint Triduana 46
Saint Venere 53
Saint Venerina 53
saints 63, 116, 118, 122, 123, 125, 131, 134
Samhain 63, 64
sanctuaries 31
sanctuary, Brigid's 44
Sanskrit 70
Satan 94, 137
Satiada (Goddess) 113
Savior 16, 47, 75, 96, 97
Savior-King, Celtic 47
Savior-Son (God) 75
saviors 127
Saxons 51, 76
Scadinauja 68
Scandinavia 52, 60, 67, 68, 70, 75, 86, 89, 122, 124
Scandinavian Goddess-worship 75
Scandinavians 52
Scath (Goddess) 59
Scatha (Goddess) 59
Scathach (Goddess) 59, 113
scholars 18, 22, 90, 91, 95
science, male-dominated 22
Scota (Goddess) 58, 113
Scotia (Goddess) 58, 113
Scotia (Scotland) 61
Scotland 6, 9, 21, 34, 45, 46, 57-61, 107, 123, 127, 142, 145, 199
Scots, the 35, 61
Scots, the Goddess-worshiping 52
Scottish Crone-Goddess 62

Scottish myth 61
Scottish tradition 60
Scottish tribes, Goddess-worshiping 62
sculptures, of prehistoric Goddess 29
sea captains, and Goddess legend 62
Sea-God, Greek 67
Sea-God, Irish 58
Sea-Goddess, Celtic 73
Sea-Goddess, Welsh 58
sea-white 49
Seabrook's Bible Dictionary (Seabrook) 140
Seabrook's Complete Encyclopedia of Deities (Seabrook) 141
sea-goddess 58, 73
Semitic Trinity 95
Senuna (Goddess) 113
Sequana (Goddess) 113
Severn River (England) 54
Sex-Goddess, Germanic 51
Sexual Love 52
sexuality 125, 131, 137, 141
Shakers 15
Shakespeare, William 42, 58
shamrock symbology 79
shamrock, Goddess' sacred plant 78, 79
shamrock, the 77, 78
Shamrock-God, Celtic 77
Shannon River (Ireland) 72
Shapely One 74
She of the White Cows 85
She Who is Born of the [Sea] Foam 52
She Who is Loved 51
She-Bear 68
Sheila na Gig (Goddess) 102, 113
Shining Father 48
Shining God 48
Shi'ites 93
shrines 31, 38, 81, 92

shrines, Irish Goddess	81
Sicily, Goddess-worship in	68
Silkie (Goddess)	113
silver	62
Sin (Goddess)	113
Sinann (Goddess)	72, 113
Sinend (Goddess)	72
Sirona (Goddess)	113
Skadalungr, Sweden	68
Skadave, Sweden	68
Skadi (Goddess)	59, 68
Skadi's Sacred Grove	68
Skadi's Temple	68
Skuld (Goddess)	68
sky	83
Skye (Scotland)	59
slanderer	94
Sleeping Beauty	35
Sliabh na Echtghe	73
Slieve Aughty (Ireland)	73
smithcraft, Goddess	41
smithcraft, in Greece	65
soil	105
Solar cross	102
Solar religion	32
Solar-Savior-Son-God (God)	96
Solar-Savior-Son-God, Jesus as	97
Solomon, King	96
solstices	35
Son-God	94
songs	141
Sophia (Goddess)	75
Souconna (Goddess)	113
south	2, 3, 10, 197
Southern hemisphere	34
space	142, 144
Spain	31, 41, 62

spirit 3, 10, 17, 42, 63, 78, 79, 81, 125, 145
Spirit of Halloween 63
spirits 76, 129
sports 32
sports, Goddess 32
Spring 2, 6, 49, 51, 63, 69, 77, 102, 140, 141
Spring Equinox 63
spring festival, Celtic 77
Spring-Goddess, Germanic 51
spring-shrine, holy 102
springs 52, 54, 55, 81
springs, holy 52
Spring-goddess 49, 51, 69
standing stones 35
Standing Stones of Callanish 35
Star 94
Star of the Sea 55, 94
star, as sacred symbol of Goddess 92, 94
star-milk 86
stars 83, 85, 86, 94, 144
star-goddesses 94
statuary, Goddess 102
statues 29
Stella Maris (Goddess) 55, 94
Stone Ring of Callanish 34, 35
Stonehenge 32-34
Stonehenge I 32
stones, three-sided 28
Strabo 27
Straight 90
Strong Fighting One 43
Sul (Goddess) 48
Sulis (Goddess) 49, 113
Sulis-Minerva (Goddess) 49
Suliviae (Goddess) 48, 113
Sumeria 86
Sumeria, Goddess-worship in 95

Sumerian Goddess-worship 75
Summer 23, 63
Summer Solstice 23, 34, 63
sun 48
Sun Father 48
Sun-God 48
Sun-God, Celtic 47
Sun-Goddess, Celtic 73
Sun/Son-god 94
Sunday 102
Supreme Being 14, 17-19, 21, 22, 28, 33, 57, 58, 90, 108
Supreme Being, female 22, 28, 57
Swan-Goddess, Irish 72
sweet girl 66
sweet nutmeat 47
Swift One 73
Switzerland 69
sword 2
symbols, Goddess 102
synonyms for the full Moon 69
Syria 38, 89, 127
Syria, King of 38
Tacitus 27, 62
Taillte (Goddess) 113
Taillten, Ireland 47
Tailltu (Goddess) 47
Taliesin 58
Tamesis (Goddess) 113
Tammuz (God) 96
Tattooed One 58
tears 11
Telo (Goddess) 113
temples 78, 92, 145
temples, Goddess 78, 92
Terrible 65
The Bible and the Law of Attraction (Seabrook) 140
The Book of Kelle (Seabrook) 16, 82, 140

The Caudills (Seabrook) 61
The Complete Dictionary of Christian Mythology (Seabrook) 141
the dead 58, 63, 116, 124, 129, 144
The Epic of Gilgamesh 143
The Goddess Dictionary of Words and Phrases (Seabrook) 140
The Goddess Encyclopedia of Secret Words (Seabrook) 141
the Mighty 91
The Unauthorized Encyclopedia of the Bible (Seabrook) 141
The Youth 90
thealogy 22
theology, male-dominated 22
thirteen standing stones 34
thirteen-month Lunar Calendar 34
Three Weird Sisters, the 42
Threefold Moon 91
threshold 63
Threshold Days 63
Tipperary, County, Ireland 73
tithing 15
Tlachtga (Goddess) 113
Tobar Bride (Goddess) 72
Tober-Bo-Finn, Ireland 85
tomb 31
tombs 31
toponymy 37
torch 139
Tower Hill (England) 39
Track of the White Cow 85
Travelers, the 53
tree groves, sacred 52
trefoil, the 77
Trefuilngid Tre-Eochair (God) 77
Trick or Treating 64
Triduana (Goddess) 45, 113
Trinity 9, 21, 41, 71, 78, 79, 91, 93, 95
Trinity (female) 41
Trinity, all-female Arabian 91

Trinity, Holy, all-male 78
Trinity, Holy, the original all-female 79
triple spiral 42, 103
Triple-Bearer of the Triple-Key 77
triple-deity 41
Triple-God, Celtic 77
Triple-Goddess 41, 42, 48, 53, 65, 77-79
Triple-Goddess archetype 42
Triple-Goddess, Welsh 58
triple-key 77
Triple-Muse-Goddess 38
triple-phallus 78
triple-phallus (of the Triple-God) 77
Triple-Goddess 41, 42, 48, 53, 57, 58, 65, 68, 74, 79
Tuatha De Danann 76
Turkey 82
Turrean (Goddess) 113
Twelve Mountains of Ebhlinne 73
twin peaks 74
Uairebhuidhe (Goddess) 113
Ugarites, Goddess-worship among 96
Underworld 67
Uni (Goddess) 70
union under the auspices of Mari 98
Unitarians 15
United Kingdom 22, 23, 37, 105
United Queendom 105
United States 135
Universe 15, 70
Vaga (Goddess) 54
Varia (Goddess) 113
veil 63
Veleda (Goddess) 113
veneration 15
Venerdì 52
Venetians, the 67
Venice, Italy 67

Venus (Goddess) 52, 53, 67, 94
Venus statues 29
Venus' Day 53
Verbeia (Goddess) 54, 113
Vikings 59, 60, 130
Virgin . . 9, 15, 42, 48, 49, 54, 66, 67, 69, 70, 75, 87, 89, 91, 93-97, 115,
117, 128
Virgin Daughter-Goddess, the 79
Virgin Mary (Goddess) 54, 66, 87, 89, 94, 95
Virgin Mary's Cult 55
Virgin Spring-Goddess, Welsh 49
Virgin, the (Goddess) 42
Virgin-Earth-Goddess 75
Virgin-Goddess 91, 93
Virgin-Goddess figure 97
Virgin-Goddess, Etruscan 70
Virgin-Goddess, Pagan 67
Virgin-Mother-Goddess, Irish 48
virgins 97
Virgin-Mother 48
virgin-mother-goddess 48
Virgo 69
Virgo (Goddess) 69
virile man 60
Viviane (Goddess) 113
Volcano-Goddess, Italian 66
vulva 33, 67, 70, 81, 103
vulva symbolism 103
Wales 21, 31, 38, 57, 107
War-Goddess 43
warrior 43, 58
Warrior-Goddess, Welsh 58
Wasp 65
water 48, 54, 61, 65, 73, 137, 141
Water Hag-Goddess 61
Water-Goddess, British 48
Water-Goddess, Celtic 48

Water-Goddess, Celto-British 54
Water-Goddess, Greek 65
waters of Sul 48
wearing of the Green, the 101
Wednesday 60
Wednesday (God Day) 60
Well Bride 72
well dressings 101
Well of the White Cow, Ireland 85
wells 45, 52, 54, 72
wells, sacred 45, 52
west 23, 131
Western culture 98
Wharfe River (England) 54
wheel 82
white 37
White Crow 52
White Goddess, the 38
White Hill (England) 39
White Lady of Death, the (Goddess) 38
White Moon 38
White Sow 58
White Witch of Clare (Goddess) 73
White-Bosomed One 52
White-face 38
White-faced 60
Whore-Madonna Complex 97
Wicce 103
Wicce, etymology of word 64
Wicces 64
wicked witch archetype, origins of 62
Wide-eyed One 69
wigle 64
wih 64
wind 32, 145
Winter 63, 135
Winter Solstice 63, 135

wisdom	21, 49, 68, 74, 120, 129, 132, 133, 135, 144
Wisdom-Goddess, Irish	74
Wisdom-Goddess, Roman	49
witan	64
witch	64, 73, 103, 128, 129, 136, 137
Witchcraft	103
Witches	64
witch's spell	58
wizard	62
Wizard of Oz	62
wizzi	64
wizzo	64
Woden (God)	60
Woden's Day	60
womb	32, 75, 81, 94
womb symbolism	32, 75
women-only shrines	44
wood	31, 75, 123, 136, 199
Worldwide Church of God	115
worldwide socio-religious culture	22
worshipers of the Crone	65
Wotan (God)	60
Wye River (England)	54
Xusigiae (Goddess)	113
Yahweh (God)	90, 95
Yahweh-Jehovah-Jove-Jupiter (God)	90
Yew Berry	73
Yoni	33, 70, 95
yoni, origin of word	70
Yorkshire, England	43
Zeus (God)	48, 90
Zodiac	94, 122

Meet the Author

Neo-Victorian scholar Lochlainn Seabrook, a descendant of the families of Alexander Hamilton Stephens, John Singleton Mosby, Edmund Winchester Rucker, and William Giles Harding, is a 7th generation Kentuckian and the most prolific and popular pro-South writer in the world today. Known by literary critics as the "new Shelby Foote" and by his fans as the "Voice of the Traditional South," he is a recipient of the prestigious Jefferson Davis Historical Gold Medal, and, as a lifelong writer, has authored and edited books ranging in topics from history, politics, and science, to nature, religion, and the paranormal.

One of the world's most popular living historians, he is a 17th generation Southerner of Appalachian heritage who descends from dozens of patriotic Revolutionary War soldiers and Confederate soldiers from Kentucky, Tennessee, North Carolina, and Virginia. A proud member of the Sons of the Confederate Veterans, he is a true Renaissance Man. Besides being an accomplished and well respected author-historian and Bible authority, he is also a Kentucky Colonel, eagle scout, screenwriter, nature, wildlife, and landscape photographer, artist, graphic designer, songwriter, film composer, musician, music producer, genealogist, former history museum docent, and a former ranch hand, zookeeper, and wrangler.

His 70 adult and children's books contain some 60,000 well-researched pages that have earned him accolades from around the globe. His works, which have sold on every continent except Antarctica, have introduced hundreds of thousands to vital facts that have been left out of our mainstream books. He has been endorsed internationally by leading experts, museum curators, award-winning historians, bestselling authors, celebrities, filmmakers, noted scientists, well regarded educators, TV show hosts and producers, renowned military artists, esteemed heritage organizations, and distinguished academicians of all races, creeds, and colors. Colonel Seabrook also holds the world record for writing the most books on Southern icon Nathan Bedford Forrest: 12.

Of northern and central European descent, he is the 6th great-grandson of the Earl of Oxford and a descendant of European royalty. His modern day cousins include: Johnny Cash, Elvis Presley, Lisa Marie Presley, Billy Ray and Miley Cyrus, Patty Loveless, Tim McGraw, Lee Ann Womack, Dolly Parton, Pat Boone, Naomi, Wynonna, and Ashley Judd, Ricky Skaggs, the Sunshine Sisters, Martha Carson, Chet Atkins, Patrick J. Buchanan, Cindy Crawford, Bertram Thomas Combs (Kentucky's 50th governor), Edith Bolling (second wife of President Woodrow Wilson), Andy Griffith, Riley Keough, George C. Scott, Robert Duvall, Reese Witherspoon, Lee Marvin, Rebecca Gayheart, and Tom Cruise.

A constitutionalist and avid gun advocate, Colonel Seabrook is the author of the international blockbuster, *Everything You Were Taught About the Civil War is Wrong, Ask a Southerner!* He lives with his wife and family in beautiful historic Middle Tennessee, the heart of the Confederacy.

For more information on the author visit

LochlainnSeabrook.com

Goddess-worship predates written history.

Meet The Cover Photographer

Billy Currie currently lives in Stirlingshire, Scotland, but originally came from a small mining village in Ayrshire. He left school at fifteen chasing a future in the music industry playing drums with a local punk rock band, but pretty soon it became apparent that music was not a viable option.

From a young age he was always much more artistic than academic but he chose the sensible route and pursued a successful career in I.T. It was this I.T. career choice that provided Billy with the financial backing to eventually be in a position to dedicate his time to his two true passions: photography and the traditional craft of wood turning.

For more information on the photographer visit

BillyCurrie.co.uk

tha gradh ag a'bhandia ort

LOCHLAINN SEABROOK ∽ 201

If you enjoyed this book you will be interested in Mr. Seabrook's other popular spiritual titles:

☛ JESUS & THE LAW OF ATTRACTION: THE BIBLE-BASED GUIDE TO CREATING PERFECT HEALTH, WEALTH, & HAPPINESS
☛ JESUS & THE GOSPEL OF Q: CHRIST'S PRE-CHRISTIAN TEACHINGS AS RECORDED IN THE NEW TESTAMENT
☛ SEABROOK'S BIBLE DICTIONARY OF TRADITIONAL & MYSTICAL CHRISTIAN DOCTRINES
☛ CHRISTMAS BEFORE CHRISTIANITY: HOW THE BIRTHDAY OF THE "SUN" BECAME THE BIRTHDAY OF THE "SON"
☛ THE BOOK OF KELLE: AN INTRODUCTION TO GODDESS-WORSHIP & THE GREAT CELTIC MOTHER-GODDESS KELLE
☛ CHRIST IS ALL & IN ALL: REDISCOVERING YOUR DIVINE NATURE & THE KINGDOM WITHIN

Available from Sea Raven Press and wherever fine books are sold

ALL OF OUR BOOK COVERS ARE AVAILABLE AS 11" X 17" POSTERS, SUITABLE FOR FRAMING.

www.ingramcontent.com/pod-product-compliance
Lightning Source LLC
Chambersburg PA
CBHW022105090426
42743CB00008B/723